Interesting Insights into the Mind

to understand one's own mind
- and that of others

Dr. Shrirang Bakhle

Become
Shakespeare
.com

First published in 2018 by

Becomeshakespeare.com
Wordit Content Design & Editing Services Pvt Ltd
Unit - 26, Building A-1, Nr Wadala RTO, Wadala (East),
Mumbai 400037, India
T:+91 8080226699

This book has been funded by WORDIT ART FUND
WORDIT ART FUND helps deserving
Authors publish their work
To apply for funding, please visit us at
becomeshakespeare.com

Author: Dr. Shrirang Bakhle
Author photo credit: Mohini Bakhle

©
ISBN : 978-93-88081-29-0

DISCLAIMER

This book is a useful fund of knowledge about the mind, its
functioning and its problems. It cannot be a substitute for
personalized care and treatment in case readers have some mental
distress or disorders. Readers are encouraged to take the help of
doctors / Mental Health Professionals if they have such problems.

This book is dedicated to

Alexander Fleming,

Who discovered Penicillin, and created the concept of antibiotics,

And

Edward Jenner,

Who created smallpox vaccine and the concept of vaccines,

And thereby saved millions and millions of lives,
Perhaps, more than any other humans in history!

Contents

Foreword

During recent decades, the world has become increasingly connected, increasingly competitive, and increasingly filled with stress. What is stress? There are many definitions, and an easy one to remember is that stress is whatever poses a challenge and requires an individual to adapt within a specific period of time.

Stress is seldom pleasant. Stress can involve working with targets and deadlines, living with ill health in a near and dear one, or coping with unpleasant neighbours. Stress does not necessarily need to be unpleasant. It can be stressful to shift to a bigger and better house in a new neighbourhood or city, to take up new responsibilities after a long awaited promotion, or even to just take care of a delightfully happy and healthy baby.

Research has shown that stress, whether pleasant or unpleasant, increases the risk of a large number of medical and psychiatric disorders. For example, stress has been implicated in conditions ranging from bronchial asthma to hypertension; and it worsens outcomes in diseases ranging from diabetes to psoriasis. Stress also increases the risk of and worsens the course and outcome of conditions such as anxiety, depression, schizophrenia, and other psychiatric illnesses.

People need to know how to buffer against stress; that is, how to prevent stress from affecting their physical and mental health. Towards this goal, a large number of approaches have been developed to improve lifestyle and foster positive mental health as preventative measures. Likewise, cognitive behavior therapy and other approaches have been developed to treat anxiety and depression, and to reduce stress, in persons who already have compromised physical and mental health.

This book, "*Interesting* Insights into the Mind", by Dr Shrirang Bakhle, a physician and counselor with three decades of experience, outlines approaches towards stress management and positive mental health. In a series of short articles, Dr Bakhle outlines mental health problems and considers simple solutions. The book is clearly written with plenty of useful examples. Readers cannot help but benefit from its contents. All that it takes is motivation, and the effort to put into practice the suggestions that Dr. Bakhle presents.

Chittaranjan Andrade, M.D.
Professor and Head, Department of
Psychopharmacology
National Institute of Mental Health and Neurosciences
Bangalore 560 029, India

Introduction

For well over three years, Dr. Shrirang Bakhle continues to be a mental health guide to the readers of The Free Press Journal newspaper that has a daily circulation of over 80,000 and millions of visitors on www.freepressjournal.in

As the former Feature Editor and the Web Editor, I commissioned a weekly article from Dr. Bakhle with a general brief that his column should focus on the complex way that a mind thinks but break it down in simple language and less of medical jargon. I also conveyed to Dr. Bakhle that writing on mental health or wellbeing was not enough. Problems needed solutions, so his articles necessarily also had to point a way out.

For me, commissioning the column from Dr. Bakhle was a small trial and I did not envisage that it would continue for well over three years and that there would be a tremendous response from readers.

The column was titled "Mind Matters" because his article gave hope and in a simple easy manner talked about the everyday issues that humans face in terms of challenges, mental meanderings and thoughts. Be it guilt, envy, depression, sadness, ego, envy, ambition, health, restlessness.. the meanderings of minds are complex. More often than not, humans tend to confuse their mind matters as a factual reality. Sometimes, they are just cognitive distortions and have nothing to do with the real world.

Dr. Bakhle's column in The Free Press Journal has evoked admiration and a sense of relief to many readers who had issues with their mental wellbeing. A candid confession is in order here. Besides the lakhs of readers, there were couple of staff members of The Free Press Journal who asked for appointment with Dr. Bakhle professionally as a therapist. In other words, mental health issues have no limitations and affect people in different age-groups and professional background.

Over the last three years, Dr. Bakhle's column has attracted the maximum response in the Weekend Supplement that is published every Sunday along with the main edition of the paper

Even though I have moved on from the newspaper, the column still continues to be read by lakhs of readers. The feedback for his column has ensured the publication of his column to date. I wish Dr. Bakhle a great future as a mental health professional and a writer besides being the excellent Physician that he is.

Regards
Ketan Tanna
Former Feature and Web Editor
The Free Press Journal

Preface

All of us were taught about heart, lungs, intestines and kidneys in school, isn't it? But were you taught about 'mind' in school: What is mind? What are the parts of mind? How does mind work? The answer is 'no'! This is in spite of the fact that mind is the most important aspect of our personality. As educated, intelligent people, we all know about diabetes, cholesterol, blockages in arteries etc. But do we have similar scientific knowledge about mind and its problems?

Mind is one thing that we keep using all the time. Right from the time you get up, to the time you fall asleep, what you are using continuously is the mind - even if you are lying down with the eyes closed - daydreaming of this and that and that!

What is it that determines whether a person will become a rock star or a shopkeeper or a saint or a terrorist? Is it the height or the size of the biceps or the skin texture? Obviously, it is the mind that decides what a person will become.

Forget achievements, what is it that determines whether a person will become happy or unhappy? It is not the colour of the eyes or the type of hair, but it is the mindset that leads to happiness or unhappiness. And, of course, the happiness and unhappiness are parts of the mind itself! So, isn't it important to know more about the mind?

That, exactly, is the aim of this book. Each article describes an interesting facet of the mind. There are more than 60 of them. Some articles describe insights about some wonderful aspects of our mind, such as creativity, curiosity, enthusiasm and adaptability. Some articles give insights about the painful aspects of the mind such as loneliness, sadness, fears, addiction and anger. But I have given not just insights into the causes of these, but also practical tips for preventing and overcoming such problems.

I have drawn on knowledge of Psychotherapies, Psychiatry, Neuroscience – and my nearly three decades of experience in treating patients. Over these years, I observed how and why some people come into the grip of unhappiness and mental disorders, how there are some common mental traps that people fall into. I also observed how some people remain happy in spite of stressful life situations and how some people successfully come out of mental distress and disorders by using counseling and medicinal treatments. These articles are the expressions of those insights.

I wish to sincerely thank Dr. Chittaranjan Andrade, one of the most knowledgeable and respected Psychiatrist teachers in India and abroad, for kindly writing the Foreword for my book.

I wish to thank Mr Ketan Tanna for many reasons. First, for inviting me on behalf of the Weekend supplement of The Free Press Journal to write this series of articles under the heading, Mind Matters. This helped me to crystallize the years of thinking into clear insights. And I wish to thank him for his kind words in the Introduction he has given for this book.

My thanks to The Free Press Journal management and specifically, Manasi Mastakar and also, Boski Gupta, for first, the opportunity to reach out to the lakhs of readers in the form of printed articles and in the FPJ website. And my thanks for giving the go-ahead for compiling the articles into this book.

I cannot thank my readers, relatives and friends enough for appreciating my articles. Their likes, after reading the articles on every Sunday, encouraged me to continue writing. And my special thanks to those readers who asked me to compile these articles in the form of a book!

Dr. Shrirang Bakhle
Chembur, Mumbai, India
Email: ss.bakhle@gmail.com
Mobile: +91-9821312013

1

You versus Problems: the boxing match

Everybody is generally happy. But the problem comes when a problem comes! And then the boxing match starts. This is a two-way match: we try to overpower and solve the problem. At the same time, the problem can harm us, make us unhappy. The problem can be anything: fear of failure in exam, financial problems, career dissatisfaction, interpersonal problems, sickness or death in the family etc.

So, what is the final outcome? Do we come out happy and strong or do we end up being unhappy (sad, fearful or angry)? It is important to recognize that most of this battle happens in our mind. And the final outcome – happiness or unhappiness – happens in the mind, too. Hence, by understanding the dynamics, we can determine the outcome.

Simple logic tells us that if we solve the problem, we will become happy. And if we are unable to solve the problem, we will become unhappy. But this isn't always the case. Suppose, someone insults you. If the person admits the mistake and apologizes, you will become happy. If the person does not do this, you will remain unhappy. Is it so?

Not always. It is possible that even if the person apologizes, you may keep remembering the unhappiness and remain unhappy for a long time. It is also possible that even if the person does not apologize, you can remain strong and get on with your life happily.

One half of this boxing match is what we do to the problem: Solve the problem, or at least reduce the severity and take steps to ensure that the problem does not recur in future.

You must have observed that some people are better at solving problems than others – problems such as exams, interpersonal problems etc. What is the difference between these two groups of people? Is it the physical strength - the size of the biceps? No. The difference is in the mindset – the attributes of the mind. If we understand these abilities, we can learn them.

The most important ability is remaining calm in the middle of problem situations. Whenever we realize that we have a problem, the first reaction is that we become unhappy - sad, fearful, angry. For example, when a student realizes that he may not do well in an exam, the first reaction is fear. However, we see many students who remain anxious for a long time – and are unable to concentrate on studies. This worsens the situation, increasing the chances of doing poorly in the exam. Hence, the first step in solving a problem is to become calm.

It is easier said than done. But it can be done. There are various techniques for removing the negative emotions; techniques that can be learnt. We will discuss them in future articles in this series.

A calm mind offers several advantages: it can think of more facets of the situation whereas the emotional mind can hold only a few facets. For example, while tackling interpersonal problems, the calm mind can think of many related events, people and different options – before deciding on an action plan. The emotional person takes decisions based on few emotional facets and hence has a less chance of tackling the problems well.

The calm person has more patience while the emotional person rushes into actions. For example, a young child is having difficulties while learning to do some activity (such as tying shoe laces). The calm person will patiently observe and teach the child. The emotional person will have an emotional outburst quickly.

The calm person has better empathy. The emotional person's mind is so clouded by the emotions that he cannot perceive what is going on in other people's minds. Hence the calm person can tackle interpersonal problems better.

The other half of the boxing match is what the problem does to you. Sometimes the problem leaves the person emotionally shaken – even if the problem gets solved. For example, a person may face the possibility of losing his job. This experience may make the person fearful or bitter – even if he manages to retain the job. This typically happens if the person keeps on brooding about the unpleasant experiences.

The person with the happy mindset understands that problems are a part of every person's life and that they are to be taken in the stride. So this person tries to learn from the problem, is happy that the problem is solved and then gets on with the life. Even if the problem is unsolvable (e.g. death of a dear one), the calm person overcomes the distress and gets back to living a productive life.

So, by acquiring the calm and happy mindset, we can tackle the problems better and not allow the problems to damage our mind.

2

What motivates you: fear or happiness?

Consider exercise (walking etc.). What drives you to do it: fear of obesity, fear of heart attack – or the wish feel fit and healthy? Interestingly, the activity is same: walking. But the motivation can be vastly different. And therefore, what happens while doing the activity can also be vastly different.

Consider a person who smokes cigarettes. He (or she) decides to quit. Will s/he be successful in giving up cigarettes permanently? Or will s/he give up for a few days – only to restart it again? The most important deciding factor will be reason for motivation: is it fear or happiness?

Suppose, this person had developed cough along with blood in the sputum. So s/he went to the doctor who suspected cancer. That put tremendous fear in the mind of the person. So s/he decided to quit smoking. But suppose, the tests came negative for cancer. A few days passed. Over time, the fear became less – and with that the motivation to quit became less intense. And so, the person starts smoking again.

Consider another person. This person is an exercising person who loves the feeling of fitness. But s/he, too, is prey to the habit of smoking. This person, too, goes through the same story of cough and suspicion of cancer. But this person loves and values his (or her) feeling of health and fitness. Once s/he realizes how the smoking is going to damage the health sooner or later, this person quits smoking. But because the motivation is "I want to remain healthy and fit", the motivation is likely to last long – even after the fear of cancer or heart attack has gone away.

There is one other problem created by the fear motivation. It leads to build up of stress. For example, consider a student who has to study for an exam. What is the motivation: fear of doing poorly in the exam or the wish to do well in exam? It is important to note that the activity is the same: studying. If fear is the motivation, then it remains in the mind as long as the study period lasts. Remaining in a fearful and unpleasant mind state for a long time is not at all good. It can lead to many other problems: loss of confidence, damage to self-esteem, irritability and disturbed concentration etc.

On the other hand if the motivation is 'doing well in the exam', the mind state is quite different – and better. Here 'doing well' may mean different things to different students. For the academically good student, it may mean topping the class. For the average student, it may mean passing comfortably. But the mindset is the same: anticipation of happiness. This feeling leads to positive emotions such as determination and enthusiasm.

Of course, fear is not always bad. Fear makes us cautious. For example, while driving, fear is a good motivation that makes us take precautions. But being fearful throughout the driving period is not good.

These opposite moods of fear and happiness affect decision-making, too. For example, the decision to change jobs, the decision to give up the job and start a business. What is the motivation: fear or the pursuit of happiness. For example, if your motivation is fear, you are unlikely to give up a secure job and start a business. But if your motivation is anticipated glory, then you may give up the job and start business.

It is important to note that fear and happiness are emotions. Once you realize that the mood is affecting the decisions, you may want to wait and change the mood to a more appropriate one and then take the decision. For example, suppose you are thinking of changing your job. Do you want to get a new job because you are 'fed up of your old job', or because you 'like the new job'? If you are in an unhappy mood, you will want to get rid of your existing job and take up whatever job is available – even if it is not so good. But if you are in a good mood, you may want to wait till a really better job becomes available.

How to make good use of the best of both methods? The fear (or anger or sadness) motivation may be a starting point. So you decide to do a particular activity that can take you from unhappiness to happiness. At that time, change the goal: from avoiding pain to becoming happier. For example, if your relationship with a person is disturbed. So you decide to do a few things (such as spending more time with the person) to remove that unpleasantness. Now, change the motivation: make the motivation 'improving the relationship' (and not 'removing unpleasantness')! You will notice how this change will make a huge difference for the better!

3

The 'muscles' of the mind!

There are so many students in a class. But only some of them have an intense determination to succeed in the exam. They will work long hours. They are willing to sacrifice many pleasures for the sake of success. And they succeed! What is the difference between them and the other students? How did they become like this?

We also know many simple people who develop depression (sadness-proneness) or develop anxiety (fear-proneness), or become anger-prone. All of us have seen normal people who gradually develop addictions. There are people who try to come out of their addictions. Some succeed, others don't. What is it that causes these changes – good or bad – in the people?

It all depends on the 'muscles' of the mind! 'Muscles' of the mind? Let us see what this means.

All of us are born with a standard set of muscles ('biceps' etc.). Some persons decide to exercise their muscles. Some people do hard manual labour. The result: stronger and bigger muscles!

On the other hand, if muscles are not used for a few weeks, they become weak and thin. For example. If you put your forearm in a plaster cast (due to fracture), within a few weeks the muscles become weak.

What about the 'muscles' of the mind? The mind is created in the brain. There are different brain circuits for different mind functions. For example, there are brain circuits for different emotions and wishes. They are the equivalent of the body's muscles. When we 'exercise' these muscles (the circuits), they become stronger. It means they become more efficient. They start responding more quickly and intensely.

For example, if you practice mathematics more, the circuits involved will become more efficient. They will respond more quickly and precisely.

It has been found that, sometimes, the brain part involved actually becomes bigger – just like the body's muscles! For example, in a study of taxi drivers in London, it was found that they have a bigger Hippocampus (a part of the brain) – as compared to normal people! This was simply because they used this part more often. This is the phenomenon called 'neuroplasticity'. It means that the wiring, circuits and cells actually become stronger – if we use them more often.

What's the use of this knowledge? It helps to understand the different examples given at the beginning of the article: Why some people develop intense determination; how normal people become depressed (prone to sadness) or anxious (prone to fear) or anger-prone; why some people develop addictions; and finally, how some people are able to overcome their addictions – while others are not.

The basic determining factor is 'how often you use a particular mind function (brain circuit). If a sportsperson thinks more often about excelling in the sport, the wish becomes stronger. Whereas, if s/he doesn't think more about 'wish to watch movies', that wish 'muscle' will become weaker!

Now comes the tug-of-war: this sportsperson is getting ready to go for practice. And a friend calls saying, "let's go for a movie". Which wish will win – the 'wish to practise' or the 'wish to go to the movie'? The 'wish to practise' has more 'muscle', so it will win.

The development of addictions and the battle to come out of the addictions are a constant tug-of-war. This is true for the 'chemical' addictions (such as alcohol and nicotine addictions), as well as other addictions such as internet addiction or gambling addiction.

A non-addict person starts thinking more and more about the wish to indulge in the addiction. In effect, s/he is exercising that 'muscle' of the mind. Over a period of time, this wish becomes stronger and more intense – as compared to other 'normal' wishes such 'wish to maintain good health', 'wish to enjoy good relationships' and the 'wish to work'. Then, in the tug-of-war between the 'addiction wish' and the normal wishes, the addiction wish (being stronger) keeps winning and becomes stronger. The person gets deeper into the addiction.

When a person wants to some out of addiction, s/he has to do the opposite: make the normal wishes stronger by thinking about them more often. And, at the same time, make the addiction wish weaker – by thinking less about it. If a wish is not recalled for a long time, it becomes weaker. Then the normal wishes start winning the tug-of-war, and finally the person comes out of the addiction.

The same principle is true for the 'emotion muscles' of the mind. If a person tries to remain happy for a long time, that brain circuit will become stronger. If s/he becomes angry or sad or fearful more often, those emotion centres will become stronger.

By remembering and using this principle, we can make different wish or emotion 'muscles' stronger or weaker – to our advantage!

4

What's the 'use' of unhappiness?

Everything in the human body has a purpose. Unhappiness -sadness, fear and anger - are the unpleasant emotions present in our mind. So how can they be useless? But then what is the 'use' of these unpleasant emotions?

When problems come, we become unhappy (sad, fearful or angry). That unhappiness motivates us to solve the problem that has caused it. For example, you find some untidy mess in your bedroom. You become unhappy. That will motivate you to go and tidy up the mess. But suppose you were not bothered about it and did not become unhappy, you will probably ignore it and not put in all the efforts to tidy it up. Thus the unhappiness has a 'use': motivating us to solve the problem that has caused the unhappiness. So, some unhappiness can be considered as essential!

We can think of the unhappy emotions – sadness, fear, anger - as watch dogs. Whenever they encounter a problem, they start barking vociferously to attract our attention towards the problem. Then the owner comes out, asks the dogs to become quiet and tackles the problem that started the pandemonium. So far, so good.

But sometimes, these unpleasant emotions become too intense, too prolonged and too dominating. They themselves become another problem – apart from the original problem that caused them. They literally cripple the thinking and functioning. And, being unpleasant, the sadness, fear and anger make the life miserable. Sometimes these can even lead to mental problems such as depression, anxiety and bitterness / anger. In the worst cases, the unpleasantness becomes so unbearable that the person contemplates ending the life to escape from the intense unpleasant brooding going on in the mind. People who contemplate suicide may blame various problems and people for the suicide. But the final cause is the intense miserable feeling in the head. If, somehow, they are able to overcome that intense unhappy emotion, they can go back to living and manage the problem in their lives.

Sometime or the other, everyone comes into the grip of sadness, fear or anger that disables the ability to think and function for some time. People get into an unpleasant 'mood' that persists for some time.

They get into the "Oh-my-god-what-a-big-problem" attitude!

Suppose, a person becomes sick. So he become unhappy. He starts thinking about all the problems associated with the situation: "Oh, no! This severe back pain had to happen now – when I have so much important work to do. That bag I took was too heavy. I won't be able to deliver that job on time. Then my boss will be very angry. Taking leave will hamper my chances of promotion." And so on and on! "I won't be able to carry my young child. Then my wife will be overburdened. I will have to take so many medicines. I hate taking medicines. I hope I don't have to get admitted." Then he thinks, "Oh, no! This back pain had to happen now ..." And then the whole unpleasant unhappy thinking cycle goes through his mind again and again! Thus, when faced with the problem, he gets into an unpleasant 'mood' and keeps on brooding about and counting all the problems.

While so much thinking is going on, he forgets to call up and visit the doctor!

This is the classic "Oh-my-god-what-a-big-problem" attitude! The person emotionally keeps on thinking again and again, "OMG, I have such a big problem! OMG, I have such a big problem!" But, he forgets to take the steps to solve the problem! So he suffers the unpleasantness of the negative emotions for a longer time and is unable to manage the problem well.

The opposite of this pattern of thinking is the "What-can-I-do-about-it?" attitude. In this, the person gets into the same problem: severe back pain. Naturally, he, too, becomes unhappy. But he manages to contain the unhappiness. The barking unpleasant emotions do their job of alerting the master. Then the master quietens them, becomes calm and takes charge of the situation. Coolly, he assesses the situation and thinks: "What can I do about it? Can I solve the problem? Can I, at least, reduce the severity of the problem? Can I take steps to prevent this problem form troubling me in future? If I cannot solve the problem, can I adapt and change myself, so that the problem doesn't trouble me emotionally?"

His whole focus is on the various steps that need to be taken. And he does it fairly calmly. So he is more efficient in minimizing the complications of the problem. This is the "What-can-I-do-about-it?" Attitude.

Whenever you feel caught in the grip of unhappiness, think: Am I doing the "OMG-what-a-big-problem!" type of thinking? Then it is time to get into the "What-can-I-do-about-it?" attitude!

5

The mind and the diet plan

All diet plans begin with a wish in the mind: the wish to become slimmer and look better. Then comes the belief: "If I lose so many kilos, I will become slimmer". Then comes the knowledge: the way to lose weight, is to eat fewer calories. And so, the battle, the tug-of-war in the mind starts!

There are some high calorie foods and there are some low calorie foods. The high calorie fattening foods are oily, fatty, sweet foods – the foods that most of us LOVE to eat! The lower calorie or lesser fattening foods are the natural healthy foods: veggies, salads, fruits, natural cereals etc.

The problem is how to eat fewer calories. We find that people follow three ways of doing it. (I am not recommending all the methods. I am discussing them because different people are already following them.) One way is to starve – simply eat less. Another way is to eat only high calorie, tasty foods and eat very less of the lower calorie, healthy foods. The last way is to avoid the high calorie foods and eat the lower calorie or natural foods. Which method do you follow?

The main culprit is an intense wish to eat lots and lots of tasty, high-calorie foods. And the point of battle is when you see that tasty dish on the table that everyone is eating. How to win that battle, that moment?

I always say that the best exercise to lose weight is 'to repeatedly move the head from right to left'! You might wonder how this small exercise can help to lose weight. The key is that this exercise should be done when you find tasty, fattening food on the dinner table! That is, say "No"! All of us educated people are aware what we are not supposed to eat. The problem is not lack of knowledge. The problem is controlling that desire – even while seeing the dish on the table.

People are always looking for magical diets prescribed by exotic dieticians. It is important to realize that the diet plan is on paper. It doesn't work unless the craving in the mind to eat lots of tasty, fattening food is controlled.

One way to win this battle is to ensure that fattening food is not present on the table! But this isn't always possible. There may be other people in the family who like those foods and can afford to eat them e.g. young children. So the foods are made for them and the dieters fall prey!

One other strong view is that if we are going to give up the pleasure of eating tasty foods, then what's the point of living. One practical solution to this is to eat only a small quantity of that food. The wish to experience the taste is fulfilled. And at the same time, we have consumed few calories. People who get satisfaction only after eating lots and lots of that dish, put on a lot of weight. Observe your mind: how much quantity of that tasty item you have to eat before you get satisfied. The solution is: fill the stomach, satisfy the hunger with other lower calorie foods and then relish the taste of the tasty dish by slowly eating a small portion of it! So you get the best of both the worlds: enjoy the taste but ingest fewer calories.

The other method that some people follow is the method of starving. If the wish to look better is intense, it can overcome the hunger wish. People start ignoring hunger pangs. But it is not a wise thing to suppress this basic instinct. Food is not poison. It is necessary for healthy living. You may feel that this is such an obvious thing, so why am I stating it. Nowadays, we see many cases of over-successful dieting! For many people, the word 'dieting' meaning 'eating less'! We come across many people, especially teenage girls, who have an intense wish to lose weight at any cost. So they start eating less and less – to the extent that they become underweight! And even at that point of time, they have the fear of becoming obese! What is happening in their minds?

The wish to eat less becomes so intense and ingrained, that these girls are unable to give it up – even after they have become underweight. The second problem is the irrational fear that if they give up starving and start eating normally, they will suddenly go from underweight to obese! They forget that they can closely monitor and maintain a normal weight. And meanwhile, because of starving and depriving the body of essential nutrients, they fall prey to illnesses such as tuberculosis or hormonal disturbances.

Thus, if you understand your mind, that diet plan will really work for you.

6

Happiness: the great equalizer!

What is the goal of your life? If you ask this question to different people, you will get different answers. Somebody's goal may be to own a wonderful house. Another may say that the goal is to get that education or promotion or so much money or good health etc. Then you ask the next question: Why do you want house or education or promotion or money or good health? The answer will be, "It will make me HAPPY."

The point to be realized is that, finally, what everyone wants in life is to become happy! Happiness is the ultimate goal of EVERYONE! People may define their happiness in terms of different wishes: wish to take good care of family, wish to enjoy different relationships, wish to help people or even, wish to kill people who don't follow one's ideology! We feel that when these wishes are fulfilled, we will BECOME HAPPY! So every day, throughout our lives, all of us work towards getting happiness.

This is true for all people – irrespective of age, gender, economic status, race, religion, nationality etc. Everyone, finally, wants happiness in life. Thus, Happiness is the great equalizer!

Happiness is an emotion that we experience in our minds. Consider the happiness of a poor person, who manages to buy a bike after a lot of hard work. He feels a lot of happiness in his mind. Now consider a rich person. He, too, puts in a lot of hard work. And then he manages to buy an expensive car. So he, too, feels a lot of happiness. The happiness that this person feels in his mind will be IDENTICAL to the happiness of the person buying the bike! Both are going to feel the same type of pride for many days. Thus the emotion of happiness is the great equalizer. The happiness – or the unhappiness – that every person experiences is the same!

What is a Happy Life? A Happy Life is full of Happy Days. So if we want a happy life, every day of our lives should be happy. When the question is asked, 'Was your day – or life – happy?', we want the answer to be an emphatic YES!

There is this old saying: Money cannot buy happiness. But there is a retort to this saying: Money can buy chocolates! So what's the truth?

If we allow ourselves to be at the mercy of wish fulfilment, then life will be a sequence of moods: happy, unhappy, happy, unhappy and so on. But what we want is a happy life, isn't it?

The key to a happy life is the Happy Attitude! Events happen in the world around us. The mind analyses all these events. If a wish is fulfilled, the mind becomes happy. If a wish is antagonized, the mind becomes unhappy. A person with the Happy Attitude takes the problems in the stride. The person knows that some problems are inevitable in every person's life. But s/he does not allow the problem and the unhappiness to dominate the mind. S/He faces the problems with a strong calmness.

The Happy Attitude does not mean laughing like a fool in the middle of problems. It means the ability to enjoy the joyful moments and the ability to face tough situations calmly.

This Happy Attitude is more powerful than the situations. It can help everyone in all situations. And anyone can learn and adopt this attitude.

On the other hand, some people become too attached to their wishes. Then if the wish is antagonized, they collapse emotionally. For example, all of us have read about people who commit suicide because of failure in exams or breaking of relationships.

The principle of 'Work for the best but be mentally prepared for the worst' is an integral part of the Happy Attitude and is essential for leading a happy life. 'Being mentally prepared for the worst' means the attitude that 'I will put in my best efforts, but if I don't succeed, it's not the end of the world. I can remain calm. And what I really want from life is happiness. That achievement is merely one of the ways of getting it'. This person realizes that there are many avenues for getting happiness. And even if the situation is tough, it is possible to face it calmly.

Thus the emotions of happiness (and unhappiness) are great equalizers. They are the same for everyone. Even if everyone's goals are different, what everyone wants, finally, is happiness.

The Happy Attitude is more powerful than tough situations. And everyone can learn the Happy Attitude and lead a happy life – irrespective of age, gender, economic condition, race, nationality or religion.

7

"... and they lived happily ever after"!!

We all have read typical fairy tales that go like this: "And then, the prince slayed the dragon, married the princess and they lived happily ever after!" We actually believe in this type of story ending – even in our life!

We tell ourselves: "Let this problem in my life get solved and then I will live happily ever after!" The problem may be anything: an unhappy marriage and divorce process, some sickness in the family, a lousy boss and so on. We are very unhappy because of the problem and desperately wish to become happy again. So we tell ourselves: once this problem is over, I will be happy.

There are many fallacies of having this attitude. The first fallacy: this statement implies that we will *not* be happy till the problem is solved. For example, consider a person who is stuck in a relatively poor job – as compared to his/her abilities or expectations. Now, this person cannot get a better job immediately. So s/he thinks: "How can I be happy when I am in this lousy job?" This person has linked his/her happiness to an outside situation. This attitude leads to more trouble. It means that s/he is helpless. S/He has no control over his/her own emotions. The happiness or unhappiness in the mind is totally under the control of situations and other people! As long as the situation remains the same, s/he will continue to be unhappy.

This is not true. We all have seen people who are happy in spite of problems. We all know people who can laugh heartily in spite of physical disabilities or other problems like poor economic condition. So it is possible to be happy in the middle of problems.

Another catch in saying, "When the problem get solved, I will become happy", is that if one problem gets solved, another may come. So then this person concludes that his/her life is a series of problems, so s/he can never be happy.

Then, is it really possible to become happy and live happily ever after? Or is it just a childhood myth? It is possible if you have the right attitude. So, what exactly is this attitude?

It is important to have a balanced and truthful attitude towards life. Just as we get problems in our life, we also get many joys in our life. People with unhappy attitude selectively think about the problems in their lives – while ignoring all the small and big joys in the life. So the balanced view is: Yes, there are problems in my life but there are joys, too".

But the most important attitude to have is to decide to be happy – in the middle of problems! First of all, we do not know if the current problem is going to be followed by another problem. So why wait to be happy. Be happy right now.

Secondly, if we look for joys, we can always find them. Then it is a matter of choosing whether you want to allow joys to dominate your mind or problems. We can choose to enjoy the pleasures – while acknowledging the problems in our life.

Being happy in spite of problems does not mean ignoring problems. It does not mean fooling oneself that there are no troubles in life. It means a rational attitude of accepting problems but choosing to focus more on the joys rather than the troubles.

Being happy in the middle of the problems also does not mean going 'ha ha ha ha' even if someone close is in trouble (such as serious sickness). It is important to remember that peace and calmness are shades of happiness, too. It is possible to be calm and peaceful even in the face of difficulties. In fact, it is desirable. A calm person can not only face problems better, s/he can tackle them better.

So, which person has a better chance of 'living happily ever after': the person who can remain happy (or calm, peaceful) in the middle of the problem situation or the person who is waiting for problem to get solved to become happy?

So we should change the fairy tale ending a little: "The prince was battling the dragon. But even when he was battling it, he was happy. The prince faced many big and small dragons in his life. But he had decided and chosen to be happy and at peace at all times. Then as a part of celebration of life and joy, the prince and princess got married and they lived happily ever after!"

8
What is the meaning of 'attitude'?

We keep using the word 'attitude' all the time. We have certain attitudes about everything: politics, religions, sports, movies and actors, friends, relatives, money, job, veg / non-veg food and so on! For example we say, "We need to change people's attitude towards HIV-affected persons". Sometimes, we say about some people: "S/he has an attitude". Attitudes form a large chunk of our minds. Also, different people can have radically different or opposing attitudes towards individual topics. And this leads to so much conflict. So attitudes are important. But what, exactly, is an 'attitude'?

An attitude is basically a Belief-Wish-Emotion Triad. What's that? For example, consider the attitudes towards the topic of God. Religious people have the 'belief' that God exists and He answers prayers. So they have the 'wish' to pray to God. And they feel the 'emotion' of happiness when they pray. Thus they have this Belief-Wish-Emotion Triad towards the God. And if we consider different religions or cults, each has a different Belief-Wish-Emotion Triad towards God.

On the other hand, atheists have a different Belief-Wish Emotion Triad. They 'believe' that God does not exist or that God does not answer prayers. So they do not have the 'wish' to pray to God. And hence they do not feel any 'emotion' of happiness when praying to God.

One can find a variety of attitudes towards almost all topics. For example, consider the attitudes towards silk. Different people have different Belief-Wish-Emotion Triads about it. Many people 'believe' that silk is wonderful to touch and wear. "It looks so rich and classy" etc. So they have the 'wish' to buy and wear silk clothes, sarees etc. And they feel the 'emotion' of happiness when wearing silk.

But the vegans and animal-lovers have a different Belief-Wish-Emotion Triad towards silk: They have the 'belief' that creating silk is cruelty because thousands of silkworms are killed to produce a single silk saree. So they have the 'wish' not to produce or wear silk. And they feel the 'emotion' of sadness when seeing silk. So they have a radically different B-W-E Triad about the topic of silk.

Thus different people have different attitudes towards all the topics. Even a single person may have different attitudes towards a particular topic at different stages of life. For example, consider cartoon films. Young kids love them: a specific B-W-E Triad. In the thirties and forties, they find the cartoon films boring: a different B-W-E Triad. Thus attitudes can change with time and experiences.

That is what all the media people understand and use. They aim to change people's attitudes towards various topics – from mobile phones brands to social issues such as farmers' suicides. Here, it is important to understand the concept of intensity of the Belief-Wish-Emotion Triads. The Emotion is a very important part of the B-W-E Triads.

The emotions can come in various intensities: mild, moderate intensity or severe intensity emotions. If the emotion is mild, the linked belief and wish also becomes mild or less important. But if the emotion is intense the entire Belief-Wish –Emotion Triad becomes intense and important.

With this knowledge, we can study how the media create B-W-E Triads of various intensities in the our minds. For example, consider an altercation between two communities in which a person dies. How will the media portray this incidence? Will it be described as 'an unfortunate incidence' or will it be portrayed as 'A TERRIBLE, COUNTRY-SHAKING EVENT'? The impact these two descriptions have on the minds of people will be quite different. In the first option, people will simply say that a bad thing has happened, discuss it and then get on with life. In the second option, people will become very emotional (angry). The intense wish will result in people taking action – revenge, more fights etc.

Can we control and change out attitudes? The trick here is to change the beliefs, wishes and emotions. For example, suppose you come to know that you have diabetes. So, what is your attitude towards it? What Belief-Wish-Emotion Triad do you have? Do you have an intense B-W-E Triad: Belief: "Diabetes is a HORRIBLE illness to have". Wish: "I REALLY, REALLY WISH I HAD NEVER GOT DIABETES". Emotion: Intense sadness and fear. Or do you have a milder B-W-E triad? Belief: "Diabetes is unpleasant, but I can lead a near-normal life". Wish: "I wish I hadn't got diabetes". Emotion: mild sadness and fear. What is the difference between the two? Conceptually both are same. It is not that one belief says that diabetes is bad while the other says that diabetes is good. But the difference is in the intensities of the words used – and the intensities of the emotions.

All of us are full of attitudes towards all the topics. It is useful to understand how people and situations influence our attitudes and how we can change our own attitudes.

9

The wrestling match between emotions in the mind

You are sitting on a roller coaster. It is about to start. You are feeling happy - and a little anxious. 10-9-8-.. It starts. First sharp swerve. You feel more anxious – and a little less fun. The next big swoop and a major fear kicks in. Happiness is almost gone – you wish you hadn't come. Then the confidence comes back. "Wow! It's great fun!" Feeling less fear and enjoying more and more. Whoosh! You are home. Enjoyed it!

We can experience emotions in various intensities: mild, medium or intense. For example, if your young child carelessly tears your newspaper, you may feel mildly angry. If s/he tears the school notebook, you will become medium level angry. But if s/he carelessly tears some important office papers, you will become very angry.

Commonly, we experience one emotion at a time – happiness, sadness, fear or anger. But, sometimes, as the roller coaster ride shows, we experience a mixture of emotions. On the roller coaster, we experience a mixture of happiness and fear. Sometimes, we feel more happy and less fearful. But sometimes, we feel more fear and less happiness.

Now, is it possible for us to feel two intense emotions at the same time? Can you be very happy and very sad at the same time? Or very angry and very happy at the same time? No, it is impossible. Although we can experience a mixture of emotions at a time, we cannot feel two intense emotions at a time. What it means is that if one emotion becomes intense, the others emotions have to become less intense.

This is the tug-of-war between emotions in the mind. As in a tug-of-war, both the sides cannot win. If one side wins, the other side has to lose. But, actually in the case of emotions it is more of a wrestling match than a tug –of-war! The emotions keep inhibiting, suppressing each other – as in a wrestling match!

Suppose, you are having 'office tension'. You are feeling very anxious about some office politics. Spouse reminds you that it is time for your favourite TV program. But you say, "I am in no mood for TV now." What is happening? Why aren't you interested in your favourite TV show?

It is the wrestling match between the emotions in your mind. And today anxiety has beaten happiness to ground. You no longer feel happy. "I am not in a mood to enjoy."

This is such a profoundly important statement. Observe any person who is feeling sad and depressed. The family members or friends try to interest this person to do some enjoyable activity such as going out for a movie or playing games etc. But, to the frustration of the dear ones, this person does not feel any happiness in doing that activity. The emotion of sadness has defeated and suppressed the happiness. "I am not in the mood to enjoy"!

Is this 'wrestling match between emotions' just a figure of speech or is it the reality? Surprisingly, it is actually the reality. If one emotion becomes intense, it can actually supress the other emotions. There are different circuits or centres in the brain for different emotions - happiness, sadness, fear and anger. Each of these centres has the ability to suppress the other emotion centres. And this is how one emotion can suppress the other emotions.

Understanding this principle, helps us to understand others "who are not in the mood to enjoy"? This is a major source of conflict between people. One person is feeling all enthu and the other person "is not in the mood"! The enthusiastic person cannot understand why is it that the person cannot enjoy the activities that s/he normally enjoys.

Understanding this principle also shows the way out. If you are feeling "not in the mood to enjoy", first understand that your happiness is being suppressed by the unhappiness (sadness, fear, anger). The way to solve this problem is to deliberately try and change the balance.

There are many ways of doing this. The best way is to consciously change the mood at the mind level. We have the innate ability to control our own emotions. Sometimes people find it difficult to change their mood. You are feeling sad, fearful or angry – and not happy at all. You can concentrate on your mind and deliberately remove the unhappiness and activate the happiness. It can be done more easily with practice.

The other way is to push yourself to do the normally enjoyable activity – even though you are "not in the mood for it". As you continue the activity, gradually you will find the balance changing: the unhappiness will become less and happiness will return. Once the happiness starts returning the activity will feel more and more enjoyable.

10
How superstitions arise in the mind

Our family was enjoying a cricket match. Indian batsmen were playing well. I noticed that my cousin is not watching. So I called her to come and watch the wonderful batting. She refused to come. She says whenever our batsmen are batting well, if she comes to watch, a batsman becomes out! She says that it has happened twice. She laughs half-heartedly, saying, "I know it is illogical to think that there is any link between me watching and batsman getting out but I don't want to take a chance."

Let us try to understand what happened – how she developed this superstition. During the earlier two matches, the batsmen were playing well and everyone was happy. Then came event 1: she came to watch. This was followed by event 2: Batsman got out. This lead to a sudden major sadness. Later, in the third match, when she was called out to watch, she remembered the two events and the intense sadness.

We humans keep trying to identify cause and effect relationships all the time. We feel that if event 2 occurs after the event 1, then event 1 could be the cause of event 2. For example, if you ate spicy food last night (event 1) and you developed stomach upset today (event 2), you may feel there is a cause-effect relationship between event 1 and event 2.

It is important to realize that in this case, the cause-effect relationship is LOGICAL. We can understand HOW the spicy food disturbed the stomach. But suppose, your friend, a shopkeeper, says that one particular neighbour is 'lucky' for him. If he sees that person in the morning, he does more business on that day. How do we know whether to call this a superstition or not? There is no LOGICAL cause –effect relationship between the two events. There is only a presumed MAGICAL cause-effect relationship between the two events. It is not possible to explain HOW the event 1 can cause event 2.

So, the first mind feature that gives rise to superstitions is believing MAGICAL cause-effect relationships. Do you believe that if a cat crosses your path when you are going out for some work, that work will not get done? There is no LOGICAL cause-effect relationship between cat crossing path and work not getting done. But if you believe in MAGICAL cause-effect relationship, then you might feel that possibly there COULD be some relationship.

But so many scientific theories start out as hypothetical hunches or feelings that may be there is some cause-effect relationship between two events. For example, Barry Marshal, a young doctor from Australia had a hunch that 'H.Pylori', a type of bacteria, causes stomach ulcers. But gastroenterologists did not believe this cause-effect relationship. Finally, as a desperate method to prove his theory, he drank a solution containing the bacteria and proved that he got stomach ulcers as a result!

This brings us to the next mind feature that gives rise to superstitions: the lack of willingness to try and prove / disprove the hunch about cause-effect relationship. A friend of mine purchased a new mobile. Then, happily, he called his father to tell him about it. It so happened that his father developed some medical complications that day and he passed away. As he sadly recalled various events that happened on that sad day, he suddenly remembered how he had made a phone call to his father from his new mobile. In his grief, he thought of a possible link between the two events. There is no obvious LOGICAL link between the calling from new mobile and the father's death. But if a MAGICAL link is considered, then ANY two events can be linked as cause and effect. So he developed this belief that, perhaps, calling someone from his new mobile can lead to the person's death.

This belief persisted for a long time because he was not willing to experiment to prove or disprove this belief. His intense fear and sadness prevented him from trying the experiment. Then I asked him to call me from his new mobile that he had purchased and kept away. He agreed to do the experiment and called me and the superstitious belief was broken.

The concept that a person is 'lucky' feels good to everyone: the person who is considered lucky and the people who have this belief. But this concept of 'lucky person' also has the negative side: some persons are considered 'unlucky' for no fault of theirs. Suppose a new a new daughter-in-law arrives and something good happens.

She is considered 'lucky'. But if second daughter-in-law arrives and some unrelated bad event happens, she is labelled as unlucky!

This is how superstitions arise and persist because of some mind features.

11
What to do if you feel like ending your life

Mr. Patil was intensely depressed because of financial problems. The intensity of the sadness was unbearable. He desperately wanted to escape from the constant mental pain. So, finally, he decided to commit suicide as a way of ending the mental pain. But he read an article that advised people thinking of suicide to postpone it by a couple of days. He did that. And it so happened that he came back from the brink and became a successful businessman to lead a long and happy life. This is a true story.

The biggest tragedy of suicide is this: just because the person is unable to bear the intense mental pain, s/he ends the life. By ending the life, the person misses out on all the wonderful things that would have happened in his/ her life had s/he lived on - like Mr. Patil did. Consider an eighteen-year old who ends his life because the girl he loves has ditched him. Consider the long life of another forty-fifty years of joys he would miss just because intense mental pain that could have ended after a few days. What a loss!

Suicide is the third leading cause of death among teenagers in the USA. Why would so many teenagers living in the land of hope feel like ending their life? Why do people commit suicide? Can we understand what goes on in the minds of people who want to end their life? What can be done to avoid this colossal tragedy?

People who are troubled by seemingly hopeless problems in the life think of suicide. But every person who faces such a problem does not end his or her life. People who experience intense unpleasant emotions (sadness, fear, anger) as a result of the problems, think of ending the life. So it is important to understand the difference between the problem situation and the intense mental pain. Every person who has a similar problem situation does not think of ending the life. Only the people who feel the intense mental pain feel like ending the life. So the real cause of suicide is not the problem but the intense mental pain.

Once we identify this target, we can find out many ways of tackling and solving the mental pain. The most important point to be remembered that the mental pain is a solvable problem. So why should a person end the whole life just because of a temporary and solvable problem?

One peculiar property of an emotional mind is exaggerated projections about the future. For example, if an emotional person develops intense pain, s/he starts thinking that this pain is going to remain for lifetime! The next conclusion is: therefore the situation is hopeless! The sensible person understands that this episode of mental pain will get over some time and s/he will get back the mental peace again.

But, how to remove the intense mental pain from the mind? Mind is like a room. If you keep all the windows and doors of the room closed for a long time, the air inside will become stale and toxic. If you open the windows, fresh air comes in and the stale air gets diluted. This is the difference between people who brood and people who keep talking to others. People who keep brooding about the same painful thoughts again and again, tend to develop intense mental pain. Whereas, people who keep talking to others do not brood about the same thoughts again and again. They keep getting fresh thoughts from all the people they talk to. And when they talk about their painful thoughts to others, they get diluted. Also, others give them different perspectives to look their problems. The idea of postponing the suicide works through this principle.

Understand that the mental pain is nothing but an intense unpleasant emotion (sadness, fear anger). The aim is to remove the unpleasant emotion and get peace and happiness. There are many techniques such as the Relaxation Technique or meditation that can help in calming down.

Examine your beliefs related to the mental pain. Many a times irrational or illogical beliefs are responsible for the mental pain. For example, someone insults you and you feel intensely unhappy. So what is the illogical belief in this? The irrational belief is, "All the people should talk to me nicely all the time". Is this going to be true for anyone? The rational belief is, "Although I like people talking to me nicely, it is possible that sometimes, some persons may talk to me unpleasantly". Correcting such illogical beliefs can remove much mental pain.

Take the help of mental health professionals to help in removing the mental pain. Counsellors, doctors, Psychiatrists understand this. They are trained to understand such problems. And they know many solutions (including medicines) to relieve the mental pain.

12

How emotions make us impatient

It is quality time between a parent and the child. The parent has bought a new game and wants to teach it to the child. It begins well. The parent hopes that the child will pick up the game fast. It doesn't happen. The parent becomes irritable. Instead of patiently explaining the steps, s/he starts scolding the child. The quality time would have been wonderful if the parent had not lost the patience. More the irritability, less the patience.

It is not just games, but teaching anything to the children (such as studies or even tying shoe laces) requires patience – lots of it. The parents know it and repent losing it. How did this parent – who began cheerfully – lose the patience?

Unhappiness (sadness, fear, anger) is unpleasant. When we experience these emotions, we don't like them. So we want escape from them as soon as possible. We would like to get rid of them from our mind – as quickly as possible. If 'teaching the child' is perceived as the source of the troubling emotion, we would like to 'get rid of' or finish the activity as soon as possible. This means loss of patience - and more trouble!

This principle is not only true for parent - child relations but also for any relationship. For example, consider the boss – employee relationship. Suppose the employee has to explain some tricky and important situation to the boss. So s/he begins with a lot of patience. But soon due to some reason (such as a nasty comment by the boss or inability of the boss to accept the situation) the employee becomes irritated. So her / his voice starts rising. This is obviously against her / his own interest. Yet the patience is lost – resulting in an outburst and a fiasco of the briefing – leading to problems for the employee. The reverse can also be true: the boss's loss of patience resulting in harm for the company.

This kind of damage harms any type of business deal. Take the simple case of a lady wanting to buy some fruits. Some offensive comment by the lady irritates the fruit seller. So he loses his patience, tells the lady to get lost and in the process loses his sale. As famous writer P. L. Deshpande observed that salesmen in saree shops are the epitome of patience! If the salesman is cool, he does not lose the patience – and finally gets the sale!

What is the meaning of 'cool'? Cool means a person who is able to keep the emotions under control for a long time. This ability to remain cool for a long time is an asset. The more cool a person is, the more patience s/he has.

Emotionality leading to losing patience is true not only for the unhappy emotions but also for the emotion of happiness. Surprised? Consider a player playing a badminton match. She is very patient. By playing long rallies with patience, she is nearing the win. But due to the excitement of anticipation of winning, she loses her patience. She starts 'going for the kill': trying to hit the winning shot too early. This leads to losing a few important points and possibly the match. Very often we realize that a game is actually a match of nerves i.e. which of the players is more cool and has more patience.

Ever wondered why a patient is called a 'patient'? A sick person is commonly emotionally upset and low on patience. There are many patients who become so impatient that they pop all the doses of medicines for the day in quick succession – in order to get well soon! So, probably, generations of doctors have been telling sick people, "Be patient! Be patient!" Whether it is healing of fractures or pregnancy, patients need to be patient. They need to be cool and control their emotions.

The famous 'Marshmallow test' done by the Stanford University is a test of how patience pays. In that test, young school kids were given two options: have a marshmallow immediately or wait for some time. If they wait, they would get a second marshmallow. Years later, those small kids who were able to wait, were shown to have performed better in school ending test, had lower substance abuse, had better social skills and generally were more successful in life. More control over emotions > more patience > more success in life!

How not to lose patience? The key is subduing emotions and preventing them from kicking out the patience. This is such an important ability that it can help in practically all facets of life: from dealing better with spouse or kids to dealing better with office colleagues, doing better in business deals, winning games and even doing more effective bargaining while shopping!

13

How the past pains continue to haunt the mind

I am in the gym, carrying a huge weight on my shoulders for a long time. After some time my back starts paining. It becomes unbearable. I start crying with pain. What would you tell me? "Why don't you throw the weight down? You yourself are holding on to the weight and you are complaining that the weight is hurting your back! Throw the weight away and you will be free."

This is exactly what happens when painful memories of past events make us feel miserable today. The past does not exist in reality today. If we remember the painful events they can trouble us; if we don't, they cannot.

There are many ways in which memories of past unhappy events continue to haunt us. One way is thinking repetitively about it.

An extreme example of this, is a mother of two children known to me. Unfortunately, one of the sons died because of some illness. It is more than three years now. But the woman continues to cry all the time. She is unable to do her work. The atmosphere in the house is miserable. The woman realizes the pain that she is inflicting on herself and her family. But she says, "How can I forget my son?" She angrily resists others' attempts to distract her. This is a typical example of the gym weight simile given at the beginning: she is holding on to the painful memories herself – and crying with pain. Thus thinking repetitively about past unhappy events leads to misery in the present.

Since the 'emotional thoughts' seem important, we keep thinking about them – sometimes for a long time after the event is over. If the emotions are intense, we keep thinking about them more and more. Repetitive thinking is like inflating a balloon: the more you think about a topic, the more important it becomes. Then the emotion attached to it becomes more and more intense. And, because the emotion becomes more intense, you think more about it! Just like an uninflated balloon, the topic may be small. But by thinking about it again and again, the balloon becomes bigger and bigger. And gradually, the emotional topic starts appearing huge and very important.

There is one other way by which past unpleasant events trouble us. That is by forming links between the problem and related situations. Suppose a person had some problem such as stage fright. It lead to tremendous fear and panic at that time. So, the emotion of fear got attached to the topic of performing on stage. Every time, the topic of performing comes to the mind, the linked fear is also recalled. And so, the person tries to avoid the situation – or even similar situations. This gradually to leads to illogical beliefs – such as 'unlucky dress', 'unlucky date', 'unlucky person' and so on. The person starts avoiding all such things – leading to a lot of discomfort. If you discuss these with person, s/he will agree that these are illogical beliefs.

Such phobias are one way by which old memories continue to haunt us.

One major reason why the past continues to torture us is the feeling that mistakes (one's own or others' mistakes) have lead to a painful event. This can cause intense distress that may last for a long time. For example, "If I had acted on time, this death could have been avoided." This type of guilty feeling has no solution. The damage is already done. So, does it mean that the person should remain miserable for the rest of the life? The important hard truth is that the only use of mistakes is to learn from them. Emotional repentance is stupidity. This is because such emotional repentance leads to new mistakes.

Visualize a person who slipped on a banana peel and fell down. He is miserable. So, he continues his walk – while looking behind at the banana peel. What will happen? He will bang into something (like a pole etc.). This becomes the second mistake that happened because he was looking behind at his past mistake.

Past events not only cause sadness and fear, but anger, too. Such continuing anger can lead to long term unhappiness. 'Forgive and forget' is a good policy – not because 'they' deserve to be forgiven – but because it is good for our mental peace!

So what's the way out? First is recognizing the damage that is being done because of excess recall of troublesome memories. Then the next step in consciously, deliberately avoiding the painful or fearful topic. Gradually, as the recall becomes less, the intensity of the emotion becomes less. Second way is to learn relaxation: become less emotional. Then, even if the topic is recalled, it will not lead to intense sadness, fear or anger.

14

How to overcome fears and phobias

J.C. is a nice 32 years old man who has a lot of friends. But he avoids helping his friends if they get injured. This is because whenever he sees blood, he gets such a tremendous fear that he simply faints. He avoids blood tests himself and does not accompany family members or friends to path labs.

B.L. is 50 years old. But his superstitious fears dominate his life and restrict his work and enjoyment. "If I make the fourth phone call of the day to any person, then that person may suffer from some calamity. If I wear a black shirt, something bad will happen to me. If I get an 'ungodly' thought while doing religious rituals, God will punish me." And so on.

There are many students who have such a tremendous fear of faring poorly in exams, that the fear actually disturbs their studies. The fear of making a silly mistake on stage and the subsequent possible ridicule, prevents many people from going on stage.

What can be done to overcome such fears? How to prevent such phobias from dampening the happiness and performance? If we understand the fears and phobias, we can deal with them better.

All such 'fears of different things' have two components: [1] the emotion of fear [2] the belief that there is something terrible. We need to change both these parts if we want to successfully remove the fear.

The belief that 'something terrible is going to happen' is the starting point of all such fears. In the examples mentioned above, there are such beliefs. 'Blood flowing from a wound is a TERRIBLE event' is the belief. The INTENSE fear is the emotion attached to it. 'If people laugh at my *possible* mistake on stage, it is a TERRIBLE event' is the belief. The INTENSE fear is the emotion attached to it. So we need to attack both these aspects.

The first thing to do is to examine whether the fear is realistic or unrealistic. For example, if you watch a horror movie that shows ghosts and then you start feeling afraid of sleeping in your bed at night, it is an unrealistic fear. If some of your family members have had heart problems and then you get the fear of getting a heart attack, it is a realistic fear. However, if you have got your heart thoroughly checked and the doctor says that the heart is absolutely fine and yet you have fear of getting a heart attack, then it is an unrealistic fear.

The way to tackle the unrealistic fear is to kick it out of the mind. Thinking and brooding about it, serves no purpose. The mind has a tendency to keep replaying emotional thoughts. So getting rid of unwanted, unrealistic beliefs may not be very simple. But, you may have to play a 'table tennis' match: you get rid of the thought > it is replayed again after some time > again you remove it from the mind and so on. Eventually you will surely succeed.

The way to tackle realistic fears is to take appropriate precautions. Suppose, you have the fear of getting cancer. Then take steps: avoid cancer-causing things such as tobacco, get yourself checked to see if you have cancer and then follow a healthy lifestyle. Many times I find people who have tremendous fears (such as this), but do not take any steps. Then they continue to languish in their fear.

Sometimes, the situation is realistic, but it is 'terribalized' by the intense emotion! For example, consider the 'fear of doing poorly in exams'. If a student, who has not studied well, gets this fear, it can be considered realistic! But if the student says that doing poorly in an exam is a TERRIBLE event and if s/he thinks of suicide, then it is 'terribalization' in action. It is an unrealistic assessment of a realistic situation – leading to intense fear.

The rational way of thinking about such a situation is: "ok, so, this is an unpleasant possibility. But even if I fare poorly, it is not the end of the world. First, I will put in the best possible efforts now. And, even if the result is not good, I can try again. Or there are so many alternative options that can be tried."

The second target for removing the fear is the emotion of fear itself. 'Calming the emotions' is very specific skill that can be learnt with practice. Suppose, you very anxious now. The goal should be become calm in the next few minutes. There are many Relaxation Techniques that can be learnt and practised for this purpose.

So, fear is useful if it motivates you into action. But if it only demoralises you, it is time to get rid of it.

15
How mood influences thinking

"Normally, I am a very calm and cool person. But I don't know what came over me yesterday. I was shouting at and scolding everyone – colleagues, husband – even children. Now I am feeling so bad about it." Everyone has gone through such experiences or at least, seen such changes in people's behaviour. This is one of the ways in which moods influence thinking. How exactly does it happen?

The emotions are produced by the Emotion Centres of the brain. At different times, different Emotion Centres are active. So at different times we are in different moods: Happy mood or unhappy mood (sad mood, angry mood or anxious mood). That mood determines how your mind works and how you will react – in many different ways.

The mood acts like a filter. Emotional events of the same emotion produce a bigger response. For example, if you are in a happy mood, every small happy event will produce a bigger smile and happiness. Suppose a college student goes to the college. As usual, his friends make fun of him (and each other). Now, will he enjoy the leg-pulling or will he become irritated? It depends on his mood at the time of going to the college. If he is in an angry mood, he will become irritated at his friends' behaviour. This will lead to angry outbursts which will make the situation more irritable.

On the other hand, if he is in a happy mood at the time of going to college, he will take his friends' leg-pulling light heartedly and will enjoy it. This enjoyment will make him happier.

Thus the pre-existing mood acts like a filter. If you are in happy mood, all the happy events will give you more joy and all the unhappy events will produce less unhappiness. As every stand-up comedian knows, once he gets the audience into a laughing mood, even minor jokes elicit considerably more laughter.

The unhappy mood, too, acts like a filter. If you are in an unhappy mood, all the small pricks of life will elicit considerably more unhappiness while joyous events will produce much less joy. For example, if you are in an unhappy mood, even small problems like 'things falling from the hand' or 'having to wait in a queue' will produce much more irritated reaction than normal. On the other hand, small joys (such as seeing beautiful flowers) will not elicit any happiness.

"How was your day today?" If someone asks you this question, what will be your answer? This answer, too, is influenced vastly by the mood. Suppose there were four happy events and four unhappy events during the day. If you were in an unhappy mood, the four happy events will produce less happiness. At the same time, the four unhappy events will generate a much more intense unhappiness. So what will be your tally for the day? Four major unhappy events and four slightly happy events. Conclusion: The day was an unhappy day! Is this the correct conclusion? For a calm person, the day would be equally happy and unhappy. But for a person with the unhappy filter, the conclusion would really be an unhappy day! And then, this conclusion itself would cause even more unhappiness!

Now, if this unhappy mood continues for many days, what would the person conclude? "My life is full of unhappiness." This is in spite of the fact that his or her life had an equal share of happy events and unhappy events. This is how people with depression conclude that their life is an unhappy life. Sometimes this erroneous conclusion makes them want to end the life.

On the other hand, we can find people who are always in a cheerful mood. Suppose this person encounters four happy events and four unhappy events in a day. Because of the filter effect, the unhappy evens will not prick the person much, while the happy events will produce a good amount of happiness. This person's conclusion: It was happy day! Thus the cheerful people find the life happy and easy.

One other peculiar property of the mind is that we think more about the emotional events (happy or unhappy) than the unemotional events. Now let us combine this fact with the abovementioned mood filter. If you are in an unhappy mood you will keep thinking more and more about the unhappy events. So you will spend more time being unhappy. But if you are in a happy mood, you will think more about the happy events – leading to more happiness!

A strangely true take-home message: Cheerful mood is not only the goal but also the means of achieving it! If we try and change our mood from unhappy to happy, it can make a vast difference in life!

16
Understanding happiness, sadness, fear and anger!

These four are the basic human emotions. These emotions are the most important part of every person's life. The fundamental aim of every person is to experience happiness – and to avoid unhappiness (sadness, fear and anger), isn't it? Each person may define his or her happiness in different terms: money, health, respect, sensual pleasures etc. But the basic aim is to become happy. This is true for all people: saints, goons or simple people like you and me. We also put in a lot of efforts throughout the life to avoid unhappiness (sadness, fear and anger).

Whether we go to work, clean the house, eat ice cream, do meditation or murder someone, all our activities are related to these emotions. The emotions rule our lives. Hence it is very important to understand how these emotions are created in our minds and what effects they have. Then we can use this knowledge to our advantage: to become happier and to minimize unhappiness (sadness, fear and anger).

There are many causes of emotions. But, commonly, the emotions are related to wish fulfilment. If a wish is fulfilled, we experience happiness. For example, if the wish to eat tasty food is fulfilled, we feel happiness. We have literally hundreds of wishes: from the wish to wear a nice shirt to the wish not to suffer in old age to the wish to enjoy music and so on and on and on!

If a wish is antagonized, we experience unhappiness (sadness, fear or anger). But when do we experience sadness or fear or anger? To understand this, let us see an example. A man is walking on the road and is hit by a vehicle. He is taken to a hospital with major injuries to his leg. The surgeon has to amputate three of his toes. The surgeon says that if the blood supply to his leg does not improve, his leg will have to be amputated. Now, let us see, how different aspects of the situation lead to different emotions.

Fear is caused by the harm that is likely to happen: possible amputation of the leg. Sadness is caused by the harm that has already been done: loss of three of his toes. Sadness is also caused by inevitable harm: if the surgeon says amputation has to be done, the man will become sad. Sadness can also be caused by the loss of happiness: "I will not be able to walk normally again."

Anger is directed at the cause of the harm: the reckless driver. Hence, this usually leads to the wish to take revenge, to hit back.

But suppose, next day the surgeon says that the blood supply is better and there is no need for amputation. This will lead to happiness: due to avoidance of the harm and due to fulfilment of the wish to walk normally.

The important point to be noted is this: The situations leading to all the emotions may be in the surroundings. And they may or may not be under our control. But the wishes, the emotions and all thinking that leads to the emotions happen in the mind and hence, they can be controlled. If we understand the mind and all these mental events, we can modify them to our advantage. We can use this knowledge to get more happiness and peace and to minimize unhappiness.

It is important to realize that there is no direct switch-wire-bulb like connection between the situation and the mind. It is not necessary that a particular situation (e.g. you stumbling on the road) will inevitably lead to unhappiness. Suppose you are in a very good mood and you stumble. You may simply get up with a little awkwardness and resume walking happily. But on the other hand, suppose you are in a foul mood and you stumble. You may get up scowling and cursing, "Who the hell ..." Note that the problem was exactly the same: stumbling. But the emotional reactions were vastly different. So what determined the difference in emotions: the situation or the different types of thinking? Thus, if we understand the mind and the thinking, we can control what the emotional reaction will be when we face problems.

The good news is this: we are not necessarily at the mercy of the situations. We can choose whether we will be happy or unhappy when facing problems – because we can understand and control the mind.

In the subsequent pieces in this series, we will see many interesting – and useful - aspects of the mind: The "my-god-what-a-big-problem" attitude versus the "what-can-I-do-about-it" attitude, the duel between you and the problem: how one affects the other, how the emotions influence thinking and many others.

17

What happens in the mind when we do meditation

A very common experience: A person feels 'stressed' because of office pressure. S/he does not know how to tackle the stress. Then someone recommends meditation. But the person is sceptical: "Does meditation really help? I have tried it earlier. It's too difficult. I couldn't concentrate my mind. There are so many types of meditations. Which one is the best or easiest?" And so on.

To understand how meditation works, we need to know what happens in the mind when we meditate. But before we learn about meditation, we need to understand what happens in our minds all the time. The mind receives inputs from many sources. It receives inputs from all the sensory organs (e.g. eyes), the memory and from the Emotion Centres in the brain. Thus the mind eceives so much information – all the time!

The 'attention of the mind' is focused on one or a few inputs at a time. This attention can be shifted from input to input. For example, right now, the attention of your mind is focused on this article. But if you wish, you can shift your attention to any of the inputs mentioned above. You can focus attention on the position of your left foot or to the sounds coming from outside.

Thus, you can control and shift your attention to any input.

The mind also receives inputs from memory. We keep remembering so many things.

The Emotion Centres of the brain are another source of inputs into the mind. The feelings of happiness, sadness, fear and anger arise from these emotion centres. Thus the mind receives inputs from the sensory organs, the memory and the emotion centres.

The many abilities of the mind:

~ Ability to control the attention of the mind. We can focus our attention on a particular input or topic or we can shift the attention away from a topic.

~ Abilities to control the Emotion centres: we can activate or inactivate the Emotion Centres. For example, suppose you are feeling angry. You can calm down voluntarily.

Similarly, we have the ability to activate emotions. Suppose you are feeling dull. Then you decide to infuse enthusiasm in your mind or 'charge up' your mind: "Come on, let's go"! What you did was activating your happiness.

What happens when we meditate?

When we meditate, we 'exercise' these abilities. By doing meditation, we get better control over these abilities. A better control of these abilities helps us not only while doing the meditation, but also throughout the day in all the different situations. Meditation is like net practice. Whenever we begin practising any skill (such as driving vehicles or playing musical instruments), initially we are unskilled. We find it very difficult to do it. We feel amazed how the experts can do it so easily and skilfully. But with practice, we get better. The same is true for meditation. Initially it seems difficult. But as you continue the practice, it becomes easier.

Meditation is basically not a religious activity but a skill building activity. People may use it for many benefits – including for religious purposes.

Types of meditation:

There are many types. The following is a broad categorization.

The first type is becoming aware of the thoughts, observing the thoughts. Normally, we get involved in the thoughts. But we can decide and observe the thoughts as they come and go - one after the other.

The second type of meditation involves creating a thought – an image or a sound and focusing the attention on it. For example, we can create an image of a serene scene in the mind. Some people hum a sound (religious or otherwise) in the mind.

Another type of meditation involves eliminating the thoughts as they arise and making the mind empty. If the mind is filled with unhappy thoughts, emptying the mind can bring a feeling of peace.

All these types of meditation involve controlling the attention of the mind – focusing it on particular thought or taking it away. Thus these types of meditation mean exercising the mind's ability to control the attention.

The abilities to subdue the unhappy emotions can be exercised by practising it during the meditation. But just calming is not enough. Calmness can be of two shades: dull calmness or pleasant calmness. Hence while meditating, it important to infuse a pleasant feeling in the mind.

Caution: Meditation means concentrating the mind. If you are suffering from recurrent intense unhappy thoughts, sometimes they can become more intense. In such situations, the opposite of concentration i.e. the method of distraction will be easier and more useful to dispel unhappy thoughts.

But if you can gradually reduce unhappiness and infuse pleasantness, then meditation is a good way of exercising and getting control of the mind's abilities.

18

"It's all psychological!"

We keep hearing this sentence many times, in different situations. A child gets stomach pain when going to school and the mother says, "It's all psychological"! The doctor tells a forty-plus man that his blood pressure is high. The man says, "I don't have a BP problem. It's all psychological – caused by work stress." A teenage girl becomes unconscious. The doctor examines her and says, "It's all psychological." A woman gets repeated headaches. The irritated husband says, "It's all psychological."

What is the meaning of this phrase? Commonly, when people hear this phrase, they conclude in their minds that 'psychological' means it is imaginary, unreal. They think, 'It is all in your head, there's nothing wrong with you'!

Yes, it is true that sometimes, the symptoms presented can be imaginary. But most of the times, we are dealing with a real problem. We need to understand where the problem is: in the mind or body or both. For understanding this, we have recognize the two-way relationship between mind and body.

Events in the mind produce changes in the body and events in the body affect the mind. So what is the meaning of 'psychological' in all this?

Sometimes we find that the body is perfectly normal. But disturbances in the mind cause disorder in the body. Consider a man who is perfectly healthy and happy. Suppose he hears a news that makes him angry. As soon as he becomes angry, the brain and body gets into a 'fight response'. One of the major effects is that the heart rate and blood pressure go up. So, this raised blood pressure was caused by mental ('psychological') events. It is important to see that the effect on the body was 'real' – and not 'imaginary'! So here "It's all psychological" means a disturbance in the body totally caused by a mind event. In this situation, if the disturbance in the mind subsides, the disturbance in the body subsides, too.

Sometimes, a person has a 'real' physical problem such as arthritis, acidity, migraine or heart problem. Although these problems are physical, they can be affected by disturbances in the mind. For example, studies have shown how negative emotions can not only worsen pain, they can increase the swelling in patients of arthritis. On the other hand, humour used as a therapy has led to reduction in pain and swelling in arthritis! Events in the mind lead to changes in a part of the brain called hypothalamus. This is a master area that controls many nerve pathways as well as hormones. So changes in the hypothalamus can lead to widespread changes in various organs of the body. The well-known 'fight or flight response' operates through this. Now, suppose a person already has a heart ailment. Now, if s/he develops a disturbance in the mind, it can cause increased heart rate. This increased heart rate can lead to worsening of his heart condition. So, here, "It's psychological" would mean a pre-existing body disorder influenced by mind events.

Sometimes, disturbances in the mind lead to severe distress and related symptoms such as depression or severe anxiety etc. Technically, we can say that "it's all psychological". We can say that 'it's all in your mind'. But often this statement is made with a subtle, unsaid tone of accusation or blaming. It is important to realize that mental disorders and stress are real problems. And that they can sometimes be beyond the person's control. For example, the case of the teenage girl mentioned in the beginning can be of this type. These problems, too, need treatment – whether it is counselling or medicines.

Lastly, it is true that sometimes the symptoms can be truly imaginary. But even in these situations, we should be careful before labelling it so. Sometimes, it really can be a clever trick to shun unpleasant duties. In the example of the child who gets stomach pain at the time of going to school, it can be a trick to avoid school in order to play computer games at home.

But before labelling it as 'imaginary', it is very important to be sure. We need to observe the pattern: Is it happening only at the time of going to school or does it happen even on holidays or while s/he is enjoying? If it happening at such times, too, then it is unlikely to be imaginary. Even if it is happening only at the time of going to school, is it only to enjoy at home – or is there any problem in the school that the child is trying to avoid? It is better to check out before labelling it as 'psychological' – meaning imaginary or unreal.

The phrase, "It's psychological" does an important function: it draws our attention to the most important aspect of the situation: the mind!

19
The scientific meaning of 'inner peace'

Happiness is of many types: the love of meeting dear ones, the laughter of jokes, the exhilaration of a dance, the satisfaction of seeing children do well, the glee of winning a match, the joy of sex, the excitement of a roller-coaster ride, the pleasure of eating tasty food, the intellectual stimulation of reading a book, the gratification of listening to music, the relief of recovering from illness and so on. Every type of happiness is unique and wonderful.

The smug satisfaction of defeating a particular opponent and the taking of revenge are somewhat negative shades of happiness.

But there is special type of happiness that can be called 'inner peace'. It is a type of quiet happiness that is free from the disturbance of the negative emotions (sadness, fear and anger). It is also different from wobbly excitement type of happiness. It is a feeling of serene calmness in the mind.

The feeling of 'peace' in the mind has to be experienced to understand the wonderful nature of it. I am not saying this to create a mystical aura of exclusivity around it, but to highlight that words cannot make you feel it. It has to be experienced – just like all the sensations and shades of emotions.

The brain has different circuits or centres for producing different emotions – happiness, sadness, fear, anger. And there are different centres for producing different shades of emotions – such as the different types of happiness described above. Our minds have the ability to control different areas of brain voluntarily. So we can activate or inactivate different emotion centres at will.

For example, suppose you are feeling slightly depressed due to some unpleasant news. After a while you realize that this is not good and you need to get back into your usual enthu mode. So you 'charge up' your mind: "Come on! Let's get into action!" And you become enthu and active again. What exactly happened? You inactivated the sadness centre and activated the happiness centre - directly at the mind level.

The feeling of 'peace' is a type happiness. So it is possible to activate that particular happiness centre if you decide to. As described earlier, the feeling of 'peace' is free from the disturbance of the negative emotions of sadness, fear and anger. So if we want to experience peace, it is necessary to quieten the negative emotions and their centres. It is also important to quieten other excitement types of happiness such as laughter.

Perhaps you may ask, "We can understand the benefits of quietening the negative emotions. But why subdue the excitement type of happiness? Isn't it quite desirable? What is so special about the 'peace' type of happiness?"

Normally, every person's life is a sequence of different emotions. Even if a person is happy now, s/he can become unhappy (sad, anxious, angry) easily. Thus the mind is cauldron of bubbly emotions. When the unpleasant negative emotions grip the mind and cause turbulence, we seek peace. Then the peace in the mind comes as a relief from the unhappy turbulence.

The feeling of peace is beautiful. So, as a type of happiness, experiencing it can become a goal by itself. But the 'peace' can also become a constant, background type of happiness. In between the waves of emotions, peace can become a good base to touch. When troubled by negative emotions, turning on the peace in the mind can bring the mind to a pleasant baseline. And then the mind can be activated to an enthu or active mode easily.

One major difference between peace and other types of happiness is that this can be created and experienced in any situation – even a stressful situation. For example, suppose someone is seriously sick. One has to wait and watch. In such a situation we can turn on the peace in the mind – but not the other types of happiness (such as the exhilaration of dance). The peace will actually help the caregiver and enable the caregiver to take better care of the patient.

Meditation is a good method to develop the ability of creating peace in the mind. During meditation, we can practise the abilities of quietening the negative emotions and activating the peace centre.

When wishes are fulfilled, we become happy. When wishes are antagonized we become unhappy. Therefore, the Buddhist philosophy prescribes renouncing: relinquishing the wishes along with the attached emotions – as a method of achieving peace. But as can be understood from this article, the key is practising the mental abilities of quietening the negative emotions and activating the emotion of peace.

One other major difference between peace and other types of happiness is that peace doesn't require any external factors such as other people or food or other pleasure-producing things. We can activate it whenever or wherever we want.

20
The infectious nature of emotions

All of us have seen this: There is a group of people who are in a sombre, serious mood. It may be a group of people who have come to see a patient. Or it may be a group of office team members who are discussing some problem. Then a person – who is known to be jovial or enthusiastic– enters the room. S/he starts talking humorously or enthusiastically and everyone starts smiling. Everyone's mood changes to happiness. It is as if the person has infected others with happiness!

Does it happen with only with happiness or with unhappiness (sadness, fear and anger), too? How does it happen? And how can we use this knowledge?

All the emotions can be infectious. Consider this common scene. There is a small road accident e.g. a car dashing and denting another car. One of the two persons is cool and calm. But the other person is very angry. He keeps shouting angrily. Soon enough, the other person loses his cool and becomes angry, too. How did it happen?

Anger is always directed at some person. Anger leads to a wish for revenge, a wish to hurt the other person. So the angry person tries to hurt the other person – verbally (and in some cases, physically). But suppose, the other person is determined to be cool. So, the angry guy is unable to hurt the cool person. But the angry guy keeps hitting the other person – verbally or otherwise – till the other person gets offended and becomes angry. Thus the angry guy manages 'to infect' the other person with his anger.

One of the reasons for this infectious nature of emotions is empathy. There are some neurons in the brain called mirror neurons. When we see another human being feeling some emotions or experiencing anything, our brain creates the same feelings in our mind. This is the empathy in action. We commonly experience this when we watch movies – especially emotion-charged movies. For example, in a movie, we see a mother crying intensely while watching a tragedy happen to her daughter. We, too, start feeling sad. Almost everyone in the movie theatre starts feeling sad. Suppose the mother in the movie becomes intensely angry at the villain. Then the viewers, too feel her anger in their minds.

As in reel life, in real life, too, we find this type of infectious sadness. For example, suppose, there is a death in a family. Some of the family members are crying. Relatives and friends start coming to meet them. Before entering the house, the relatives / friends are calm. But when they enter the house and see the family members crying, they, too start crying. Thus the emotion of sadness spreads from person to person just like an infectious illness.

What is the use of knowing this infectious nature of the emotions? This knowledge helps us in understanding the interaction in both the directions: How others' emotions can infect us and how our emotions can infect them. We can then use this knowledge to modify the interactions in a useful way.

For example, we find that one person in the family is very angry. By knowing the infectious nature of emotions, we can expect this person to infect other people in the family with anger. The best solution to this problem, of course, is 'cooling down' the angry person. But if this is not possible, we can actually try and keep a distance between the angry person and others. Perhaps we can try and take the angry person out of the room. One other thing we can do, is to fortify the calmness of the people who are still calm. If we are unable to control this 'epidemic' of anger, soon everyone becomes angry and the situation can go out of control. Thus, understanding the infectious nature of emotions helps us to pre-empt and prevent 'epidemics'!

On the other hand, we would like to start and spread an epidemic of happiness, isn't it? Suppose there is a group of people in a housing society or a housing colony who are trying to make plans for some function. Somehow, everyone is in a dull mood. If you want, you can infuse enthusiasm in the group by becoming enthusiastic yourself. If you start talking enthusiastically and optimistically, soon others will catch the infection and will become enthusiastic!

In a party or other groups, you find people gathering around an enthusiastic or humorous person. This is because everyone would love to catch the infection from her or him!

Thus, by understanding this infectious nature of emotions, you may be able to prevent epidemics of unhappiness. On the other, you can spread an epidemic of happiness, humour and good cheer! All the best to you for that!

21
Habits: wanted and unwanted

You are passing by the dinner table. You notice a beautiful box of delicious-looking sweets. Unthinkingly, you open the box and pick up a large chunk. In no time, it has disappeared down your throat. You go ahead as if nothing has happened. Then, after a few moments, lightning strikes, "Oh, no! I am supposed to be on a diet. I had decided not to eat such sweets." Remorse, remorse! But it is of no use. Master Habit has ruled over the slave man - again!

On the other hand, new habits may be difficult to form. You decide to go for a walk in the evening. You come back from office and get involved in the matters at home. Late at night, the guilty realization: "I just forgot about the walk." It is not easy to form new, wanted habits.

What, exactly, are habits? A habit is always related to a situation. When that particular situation comes, we respond in a typical manner - automatically, unthinkingly. This happens again and again. For example, consider the simple daily routine after waking up: washroom, brush, wash the face, go to the kitchen etc. This is habit in action.

A habit has advantages and disadvantages. The advantage is that when a habit develops, we don't have to think about what response to give, what sequence we need to follow. For example, when a person has become good at driving, s/he doesn't have to think about the sequence of movements necessary for driving: how to slow down, accelerate, navigate etc. We respond to those typical situations automatically, unthinkingly – even while talking to fellow passengers. We don't have to think and plan every movement of the hands and feet. This is a great advantage because we can do two activities simultaneously.

On the other hand, the disadvantage is that we become slave of habits. Even if we don't want a particular habit, many a times we cannot help it. Habits die hard. When the particular situation comes, we respond habitually. For example, consider a person who is addicted to alcohol and consumes it daily in the evening. Suppose, this person gets into major health problems because of alcohol. So he decides to give up alcohol. Yet, when evening comes, the habit pulls him to the alcohol. A tug of war starts in his mind: wish to give up alcohol versus the wish to consume. The habit dominates and he drinks – leading to a worsening of his health problem.

The basic issue about habits is that they dominate the decision-making process. Sometimes, the domination is so complete that we do not even realize that there is some decision-making involved. For example, consider mobile use. The situation: feeling bored or simply the realization that we have a few minutes of free time. Most of us simply open the mobile, switch on some social medium such whatsapp and dive into it.

A typical situation that I encounter often: Husband and wife enter my cabin for consultation for some important medical problem of the wife. Initially, the husband is attentive and involved. After a few moments, I start asking some questions to the wife. Quickly, the husband realizes that he doesn't have to pay attention for a few brief moments now. Immediately, the mobile gets opened, the husband starts reading or typing something – till the irritated wife or me draw him back into the conversation! This is not only true for husbands, but even for wives or even mothers of kids! Situation: a few brief moments free. The habit: immediately open whatsapp or facebook.

If we want to remove an unwanted habit, we need to introduce planning and decision-making into it. Suppose the problem is addiction. The addiction may be to chemicals such alcohol or nicotine. Or the addiction may be to computer games or mobile games. When the typical situation arrives, immediately your addiction kicks in and you start indulging in it. How to go about overcoming such addictions? The first thing is to recognize the sequence of events. The second is to recognize your typical response: indulging in the addiction. The third thing to do is to plan a different response: how you will refuse the addiction and get on with some other activity. And then rehearse this in your mind many times. So, when the situation arrives, you will not respond habitually but with a planned, wanted response. For example, the typical situation is that you see a smoker smoking cigarette, you immediately get a craving and go have a cigarette yourself. You can plan and rehearse a different response: how you will overcome the craving and do some other activity.

Developing some wanted habits requires similar steps: planning and rehearsing how you will respond to the typical situation in a different way.

22

How would you like your mind to be?

We see so many people around us. We keep meeting so many personalities. Every personality has many different features. Sometimes, we like a particular feature of a person's personality or mindset. For example, you may wish that you could be as bold as that person: "He has no stage fright. He talks so coolly, easily, fluently on stage in front of audience. I wish I could do that." Or you may feel that Mrs. A. is so caring, loving – not only for her family but towards everyone around her. Or you may observe that Mr. B. is always so enthusiastic and cheery. And you wish you could be like him.

On the other hand, you may dislike a particular mind feature of Mrs. C.: she is always in an irritated mood. So you don't want to be like her. And so on.

On the other hand, all of us keep noting how our own mind is: our good mind features (that we are happy to be having) and the bad mind features (that we would like to get rid of). One person may like to get rid of the constant anxiety, another may want to remove the sadness. Somebody may want to develop more concentration and reduce distractibility. Another may desire boldness when dealing with people. And so on.

How to bring about these changes in our minds? One way is to work on the negatives and try and reduce them. The other way is to develop the positive features. This second method is generally easier and more effective. Let us see how to go about it.

"You cannot reach a town, if you don't know where you want to go!" "On the other hand, if you keep thinking about the same town that you are currently in, you will remain there!"

Very simple and profound principle – especially when we think about the mind. Many of us are troubled by different unwanted mind features. A basic human tendency is to keep thinking about our problems – in order to solve them. But frequently, we keep thinking about the problem ineffectively, without producing any solutions. For example, a person may keep brooding endlessly about the prolonged sad mood that s/he is suffering from. And so the person continues to remain stuck in that mood. This is the principle of 'if you keep thinking about the town you are in, you will remain there'.

If you want leave that town, then you must know where to go! If you want a new mind, you must know how it looks like! Only then you will reach there.

So the first thing is having a clear picture of how your mind should be. My mind should be happy, full of peace, humorous etc. etc. Make a list of all the mind features you desire: calm, enthu, fast & efficient, active, naughty, funny, loving, caring, sharp and street smart and so on. Every person will have her or his own list of desirable mind features.

Put that list where you can see it often: in your mobile or wallet etc. Then keep seeing the list often – many times a day. It is not enough to read the list. It is important to FEEL every mind feature that you want. For example, you want more enthusiasm in your mind. Then it is not enough to read the word enthusiasm, but it is necessary to FEEL the enthusiasm. Spend a few moments feeling the enthusiasm, practising the enthusiasm.

Sometimes it is easier to observe the body actions while working on the mind. For example, if you want be enthusiastic, talk like an enthu person, walk like an enthu person. The volume, the speed or the tone of speech of an enthu person is quite different from the speech of an unenthusiastic person. So try and create that enthu speech and you will be able to bring enthusiasm into the mind.

This brings us to another simple method of developing desirable mind features: mimicking people. We observe and like certain features of certain people. One simple way of acquiring those features is to observe and mimic and learn them. For example, suppose your problem is that you panic when a problem crops up suddenly. But you know a colleague in your office who is always cool and calm when facing problems. So observe that person when s/he is facing the problems: how s/he listens, how s/he pauses before talking, how s/he talks slowly and unhurriedly etc. If you think about that person's responses, one day you will be able to respond calmly like that person.

So, rather than wasting time thinking about the problems in your mind, think about how your mind should be. Which town are planning to go to?

23
How the mind takes decisions

Every day, so many times a day, we keep taking decisions. They may be small decisions. For example, whether to follow the diet or to eat that sweet; whether to go home early or work till late; whether to buy that expensive dress or the more economical dress etc. Or the decisions may be big: whether to take up this job or that job; marry this person or that person; whether to invest in a large property / business or not etc.

Taking decisions is a tricky business. Many a times, we keep agonizing over what decision to take – sometimes for a long time. This leads to a lot of stress. Sometimes, we repent having taken a decision. For example, we decide to give punishment to our child but repent it later. And we are not able to follow up on some of the decisions. A classic example is the typical New Year Resolution.

So, decision-making is a very common and important part of our lives. But what exactly is a 'decision'? how do we know whether to take this decision or that decision? Why do we repent decisions sometimes?

Each of us has literally hundreds of wishes: many wishes related to our relationships, appearance, health, food, home, entertainment and so on. All these wishes cannot be fulfilled. There are situations when, if we fulfil one wish, another gets antagonized. For example, you have a few hours free on Saturday evening. You can use them either for working or for enjoying. You cannot do both. So you have to take a decision whether to fulfil the 'wish to work' or 'wish to enjoy'. Finally, the decision itself means the wish you have chosen. The wish then guides our actions to get it fulfilled.

How do we decide which wish to choose? For example, you have to take a decision i. e. choose between 'wish to save money' versus 'wish to go on an expensive vacation'. How do you decide?

Here we need to understand the concept of 'intensity' of the wishes. Some wishes are more intense than others. For example, if you compare 'wish to give expensive treatment to our seriously sick child' versus 'wish to save money', the 'wish to give treatment' will be more intense.

But it is important to note that the intensity of a wish can change over time and with different circumstances. For example, you have an intense 'wish to do some important work'. As compared to this, the 'wish to watch TV' is less intense. So you start doing your work. But after some time. You get bored. Now the 'wish to work' has become less intense. Then the 'wish to go to movie' seems relatively more intense. So you put the work aside and switch on the TV.

Thus decision-making is a type tug-of-war between two or more wishes. The more intense wish wins the war. And that wish becomes the decision taken. But sometimes this tug-of-war is dynamic and changeable. If the intensities of the wishes change the decision can go in other wish's favour.

This brings us to the problem of the New Year Resolutions (and so many other resolutions)! On the night of 31st December the wish to lose weight becomes intense.. During this time, suppose you are sitting at the dinner table and you have to take a decision whether to eat that oily recipe or not. Now the 'Resolution wish' is intense, so it wins the tug-of-war with the 'wish to eat it' easily. A few days down the line, as you continue to encounter delicious high fat dishes, the intensity of the Resolution wish goes down. Then Resolution wish being less intense than the 'wish to eat', loses the tug of war.

There are some decisions that are single point decisions. For example, decision to buy this expensive house or that expensive house. Once the decision is taken, it is all over.

However, there are some decisions that have to be taken repeatedly – like the decision to avoid fattening food, to exercise regularly, decision to avoid smoking / drinking etc.

Here the main problem is maintaining the intensity of the wish for long time by motivating oneself. That is why it is said that 'motivation is like bath – you have to take it daily'! This is the point of difference between achievers who are able to achieve long term goals and those who are not.

Repenting a decision can come because of two reasons: either because of change in intensity of wishes as described earlier or because of new information not known at the time of decision. However it is important to remember that the decision seemed right at that time. So stop cursing yourself for that decision now.

Wish you Happy Decision Making!

24
Dealing with Uncertainty of the Future

"Will I get admission into the college that I want?", "Will I get the job I want?", "Will I lose my job?", "Will I get heart attack or cancer?", "Will my daughter go off and marry an 'unsuitable' boy?", "Is my marriage going to end in divorce?"

All of us keep having worries about what the future holds for us. The uncertainty of what is going to happen in the future is a major source of stress and anxiety for everyone. We humans have an ability to make projections about the future. This ability has helped humans to make great progress. But, it is also a source of fear.

The anxiety creates problems in many ways. The first problem is that it colours our predictions about the future. For example, suppose, a student's preparation for the exam is not very good. Both, passing and failing are possibilities. Now the mood of the student will influence his judgment about what is going to happen. If the student is in a sad or fearful mood, s/he is likely to believe that s/he is going to fail. In fact, we see many students whose preparation is actually good, their prior record is good. But if they become depressed or anxious, they start believing in the worst outcome. This irrational prediction actually worsens the mood.

This leads to the next problem: inability to function properly. The student is unable to concentrate on studies. The employee cannot focus on work. So the negative prediction becomes a self-fulfilling prophecy: the bad mood increases the chance of the negative outcome! Also, worrying anxiously – without putting in proper efforts – leads us nowhere.

The thought that 'I have NO control over my future' is a major part of the future-related fear and sadness. But the most important point to be realized is that there is, really, a lot we can do to shape our future.

What are all the things that we can do to shape the future and reduce the uncertainty? The first thing to do is to become calm. A calm mind is far more efficient than an anxious or sad mind. So put in efforts to cool down and get the right mindset.

Secondly, get more knowledge about the problem. Talk to experts in the field and others who have successfully faced similar problems. And then convert that knowledge into action.

For example, suppose your friend has died of a heart attack. So you are worried whether you are going the same way. What can you do about it? A lot, actually. You can take many precautions to avoid the heart attack. First, get to know where you stand. Go to a doctor. Get tests done. You will come to know if you have any blockages. Learn more about your problem. Then start the treatment. Take medicines, follow a diet, relax! Get into a healthier lifestyle.

Your chances of getting a heart attack will reduce drastically.

This type of proactive efforts can help to tackle most of the uncertainties of the future. If you are worried about loss of job, you can do many things: try and improve relations in the office – with boss and colleagues, get more knowledge or skills, talk to people to learn what they are doing and so on. You can also look for some other job as a part of the effort to tackle uncertainty.

But suppose, in spite of the best efforts, the results do not seem favourable. That is the time to mentally prepare oneself. What, exactly, is this 'mental preparation'? Every person needs to become mentally strong when facing problems. What kind of an emotional reaction would you like to give when faced with problems: break down and collapse emotionally or face the problems bravely while maintaining your poise? The bravehearts face the problems better, put in the best possible efforts, help others more and recover to get on with life.

If you want to give this type of a brave response, then you must prepare for it. Decide, "Even if the result is negative, I am going to face it calmly and stoically".

In fact, we find that if a person has this calm attitude, the outcome is better. We all have seen sports matches where a player is about to lose. But the player does not lose her/his composure and coolly fights back to win the match! It is possible to learn this attitude.

The older saying was 'hope for the best and be prepared for the worst'. A better version of the saying is: Cool down, get knowledge, put in lots of efforts for the best – and be mentally prepared for the worst! There is a lot you can do!

25

Do you keep comparing yourself with others?

"Bhalaa uski kameez meri kameez se safed kaise?" goes the ad of a clothes detergent! Comparison with others is so integral and important part of our lives that we keep doing all the time. We learn about comparison right from the first day of nursery school: "See, that Neha is not crying. Then why are you crying?" And then the comparison continues throughout the life – right up to the choice of tombstones!

We keep comparing ourselves with 'others'. As a person, we keep comparing with whom we consider as our peers – our classmates, neighbours, office colleagues, cousins. Our comparisons continue – comparing our family with other families, our community with other communities, our company with other companies and even our nation with other nations!

The ad agencies are aware of the tremendous importance of comparison (and jealousy) in our mind. So many of the ads are nothing but a demo of comparison – whether it is a deo or a house.

Is comparison with others good or bad? It can be either – depending on your attitude. For example, a competition is a place for direct comparison. Is it good or bad? It depends on how you look at it: whether you want to win – or defeat others! A healthy competition is good. It encourages every participant to perform better and better. If there is no competition, people would probably put in much less efforts. Consider all the athletes. If they had to run just for personal pleasure, they would not put in so much effort as when they need to compete and win.

So the comparison in a competition is good if it motivates everyone to practise more and excel. But the main flipside of a competition is the stress it can produce – if you have the wrong attitude. There is this joke: a neta was speaking at the prize distribution ceremony of a football tournament. He said, "I feel sad that only one team won the first prize. I want to tell the organizers to ensure that next year more number of teams win the first prize"!

Every person cannot win every time. So what effect does 'not winning' have on you? If the sadness motivates you to work harder and become better, then the competition is good for you. If the 'not winning' pushes you into depression, then you need to change the attitude.

Perhaps the most beneficial effect of comparison with others is learning from others. But for this benefit, we need to have the learning attitude. If we find someone doing better than us, the immediate reaction should be: what can I learn from this person? Rather than burning in the self-created fire of envy, it useful to spend time observing what different skills or materials the person has.

Suppose the issue is promotion given to another person. You angrily feel that this person does not have any special skills but only by playing office politics, s/he has got the promotion. So what can you learn from this person? Of course, the skill of playing politics, the skill to convince the bosses to give promotion!

Healthy competition that motivates us to excel is good. Comparison with a view of learning from others is useful. But comparison with others and feeling sad about being behind is a fairly silly idea. There are many reasons for this statement.

Every person's personality and life has hundreds of facets: money, health, looks, family life, responsibilities, sacrifices, assets etc. Hence every person's life is completely different. Even the lives of siblings in a family are completely different. Hence taking a scale and comparing yourself with another person about one particular facet is illogical.

Secondly, for every such scale there will be people ahead of you and there will be people behind you. If you compare yourself with people ahead of you, you will become sad. Whereas, if you compare yourself with people behind you will feel better. So in the end what will you feel? Trying to make progress and improve one's life is a good idea. But trying to beat somebody in a life's race is fairly silly idea.

There are some happy people who are content with their life. But they feel happy to help others who are less fortunate than them. They feel happy to see everyone progressing. This is the best type of comparison with others.

Thus, comparison with others is integral – almost unavoidable. If that comparison motivates you to try and excel, it is good. If you compare notes with a view of learning, it is useful. If you compare with a view of helping the less fortunate, it is nice. But if you compare yourself with people ahead of you (about a particular facet) and feel sad about it, it is fairly silly.

26
People who take care of the chronically ill

"I love my father. He has taken so much care of me as a child. So, now I want to take care of him when he is old and sick. But, my job's demands and my family's needs and also, the negative comments of my relatives create so much stress that I think I am going become sick."

Most of the caring, loving people, who want to take care of their chronically ill dear ones, go through these kinds of stresses. The chronically ill people may not be only elderlies but even younger persons who, unfortunately, have got a chronic ailment that incapacitates them. It may mean a differently abled child or a spouse who has become nearly bedridden because of paralysis or some dear one whose mental functioning is impaired.

The caregivers go through many kinds of stresses. The most troublesome is, 'I am not able to do enough or as much I would like to'. There is always something more that can be done: more detailed nursing care, more time for improving quality of life etc. But the point to be remembered is that there is nothing like 'the perfect care'! We can keep on improving what we are already doing but, finally, we need to understand that resources such time, money and energy are limited. They need to be divided among all the activities we want to do. We have to do rationing of all these to achieve reasonable care of all aspects of our lives. With this understanding, we can do more peaceful allocation of resources.

People who live away from the chronically ill have to depend on others – professionals such as nurses or ayaahs or sometimes the neighbours. Getting work done through others is a stress - as any manager knows. As Mrs. P. V., residing in the US and having parents who live in India, was saying, "My parents are so totally dependent on the domestic help-cum-nurses that I cannot afford to offend them."

But the most troublesome stress is the stress of the Pigeon Shit Syndrome! As every caregiver knows, there are some so-called well-wishers: relatives or neighbours or known people who come only to pass negative comments on the care being given to the chronically ill. They, themselves, will not give an iota of help. But they will just criticize and go. It is just like a pigeon who will simply come and shit on your head and fly away – leaving you to clean up the mess! Beware and be cool. Do not allow such people to destroy the peace of your mind – and also the relation between you and the chronically person.

Sometimes, the sheer duration of the chronic ailment plus the ups and downs, tests the mental stamina of the caregiver. We always hope for a cure during all illnesses. But hope and despair mark the care of the chronically ill. For the caregiver, acceptance of the chronic nature of the problem is the first step in achieving peace. Taking a calm, bird's eye view of the nature of the ailment and understanding the ups and downs is essential. Mr. S. D. would feel frustrated when his wife would need repeated hospitalizations for her kidney problem. But once he understood the long term course of the ailment, he has become quite calm now. He now takes the frequent hospital admissions and dialysis in his stride.

Understanding the long term nature of the problem can help the caregiver to be mentally prepared. But on the other hand, sometimes, thinking about it places a heavy weight in the minds of the caregivers. The burden seems too heavy to lift. At that time, it is important to decide and take one day at a time. This frees up the mind and makes it lighter.

It is very important for the caregiver to good care of herself/ himself – both physically and mentally. Sacrifice is a very important part of our psyche. Caring, loving people often ignore their own mental and physical problems while taking care of the dear ones. It is important to remember that if they have good physical and mental health, they can better care of the ill ones and others. Taking care means getting enough rest, doing exercises, taking proper check-ups and treatment. It also means relaxing mentally. One should not feel guilty to enjoy entertainment or even small vacations – even if there is a chronically ill dear one at home.

The most important ingredient in the care of the chronically ill is love. It is the love for the dear one that motivates the caregiver to put in the long term care. It is very, very important for the ill person and the others around to recognize the love behind all the care.

27
How to 'cheer up' when feeling unhappy

Every day, many times in a day, we become unhappy. Getting late for work: we become anxious. People do not do what we have told them to do: we become angry. We hear a bad news: we become sad. And so on. But commonly we recover from that unhappiness - sadness, fear or anger – quickly and get on with life. But sometimes, we or people around us come into the grip of unhappy mood that is difficult to come out of. All of us have experienced or seen these kind of 'blues' that persist for hours or days or sometimes for months.

So, what can we (or others) do, to shake off such unhappiness and become cheerful or at least calm again? If you ask this question to people, you will get many types of instant advice: "Don't worry, be happy", "Take a vacation", "Do yoga", "Drown the blues in alcohol" and so on! Some types of advice appeal to us, some type don't. Some advice is easy to follow, some advice is not. For example, If you are anxious about some important forthcoming activities in office, you cannot 'take a vacation'!

This article describes many types of activities that can help us to remove the unhappy mood and become happy again. There are many methods that can be used in different situations. The article systematically describes how each method works, so we can use each method wisely.

There are two categories of methods: Direct mind-level methods and indirect methods of getting happiness. There are advantages and disadvantages of both.

The indirect methods work with a simple logic: do some enjoyable or relaxing activity and become happy. For example, 'eat ice cream', 'listen to music', 'have sex', 'read something interesting', 'dance' and so on. When we do such pleasurable or relaxing activity, we become happier. And as a result, the unhappiness becomes less. The advantage of using these methods is that they are easy to follow: eating sweets is much easier than doing meditation (a direct type method)! However, these methods cannot be used anywhere, anytime. You cannot suddenly start dancing in your office! Or you cannot tell a person to eat sweets to come out of sadness caused by a death in the family. Also, sometimes you may get a feeling that you are ignoring the real problem while 'enjoying'. But, if appropriate, these methods are easy methods that can help us to become happier.

Then there are direct methods that work at the mind level. All the thinking that leads to unhappiness happens in the mind. And the unhappiness (sadness, fear, anger) itself happens in the mind. Thus these direct methods directly tackle the problem at the mind level. If used effectively, these methods are extremely useful anytime, anywhere.

Changing beliefs about the problem and unhappiness: For example, a dear two-year old child gets a cut in the finger and all hell breaks loose! The mother starts crying, father becomes angry, grandparents become upset. Here the belief is: "Such a small child has a cut. It is such a terrible, horrible thing to happen!" Thinking calmly, the problem can be seen from a different perspective. The grade of severity of the problem needs to be understood: Is the problem a 'scratch level problem' or a 'fracture level problem' or a 'cancer' level problem? Once the belief changes, the unhappiness reduces and people become calm again. Many a times, we 'terribalize' the problem and become intensely unhappy. On the other hand, when we see how bravely others are facing much bigger problems (such as cancer), we realize that our problem is much smaller.

Changing the too-intense wishes: Failure in love or failure in exams are major causes of suicides in teenagers. "I must get the other person's love, otherwise it is not worth living" or "I must pass in the exam, otherwise there is no hope in life" are too intense wishes that can lead to the grip of unhappiness if unfulfilled. Reducing the intensity of the wish or saying that 'if wish is fulfilled, I will be happy, but if wish is not fulfilled I won't breakdown" helps to reduce the unhappiness and become calm again.

There are many more methods of cooling down the raging unhappy emotions in the mind and becoming happy or at least calm again – from simple methods such as distraction to relaxation techniques (including yoga and meditation) to taking medicines – and the not-recommended methods of using drugs or alcohol. The forthcoming second part of this article will discuss all these methods in detail. The most important take-home message is this: even if you are in the grip of seemingly unshakeable unhappiness, don't despair: there are lots of methods that can make you happy again!

28
What happens in the mind when we play games

It is highly enjoyable to watch kittens playing. When the kittens grow up and become stronger, bolder – and naughtier – the games start. The most popular games are Police-n-thieves, Football (cum 'Catch the mouse' game) and, of course, wrestling! Just like there are game periods in the school day, the kittens, too, have their game hours. In Police-n-thieves, one kitten becomes the naughty thief and deliberately bumps into the Police kitten and runs away. The Police kitten gets the idea and the chase starts in all earnest. Sometimes the Police kitten catches the thief, sometimes not. And when caught, the next game of wrestling begins. The intensity is such that for a novice audience, it seems like a fight unto death between sworn enemies! It does lead to some bitter feelings between the kittens – but only for a short while. End of the game and all bitterness is forgotten and they become chummy and soon curl up on to each other to go to sleep!

Many of the mammal kids play games. Playing games is a basic instinct that humans have inherited from the animal ancestors. And if it has been passed on as a part of evolutionary process, it must be quite useful. The most important impact is that it prepares the young ones for the adult life of living out in the jungle. The benefits are so many – physical and mental. The physical benefits are obvious. The kids become stronger. The four 'S's develop: speed, strength, skill and stamina!

But the benefits for the mind are tremendous. The first benefit is that it develops the spirit of excellence – the desire to perform better and better. A beginner starts playing and enjoying a game and soon the bug bites. S/he sees other masters playing and the burning desire to play as good as the masters develops. The importance of practising becomes easily apparent. The more one practises, the more the game improves. This leads to a long term determination. This is because although the game keeps improving steadily with each session of practice, you cannot become master in a day. Once this spirit of ambition takes root in the mind, it helps the person throughout the life –in all fields of life.

Of course, a very important part of playing games is that they are enjoyable. All games – physical games such as football or mental games such as chess – are enjoyable. The development of skills and then using the skills to outwit the opponent in the game leads to a lot of happiness.

Everyone cannot become Olympic champions. But the games give us many, many opportunities for happiness and winning. All of us keep and cherish the small medals or certificates we won in school and college days. Almost everyone can tell a story of how s/he came back from the verge of defeat to finally win the tough game. Champions keep getting made – at the housing society level, class level, school level, district level – and then at the state, national and international level. There are so many champions in so many games out there! So many champions who still remember their days of glory with pride!

The mental games give us a lot of joy, but the physical games actually lead to release of endorphins in the brain. Endorphins are the 'feel good' brain chemicals of happiness and satisfaction. They are also known to be natural painkillers. The elders, who have chronic pains, find that their pain reduces or even vanishes after playing games!

An essential part of all games are rules! The rules of a game are a sign of civilized behaviour. They allow the channelling of energy – within limits! They allow winning and defeating without actually breaking down a person. The games also give the opportunity to go back, become better and more skilled - and have another shot at it. The joy of winning and unhappiness of defeat act as motivators for doing better – provided you have the correct, positive attitude. A negative attitude will lead to unnecessary bitterness.

The team sports have unique benefits. To win, all team members have to play in coordination with each other. We have to curtail our egos to become a part of a winning team. And that is no small benefit! The bonding that develops from being together for a long time, cooperating with each other for a common goal, helping each other to do better and finally, celebrating with each other leads to a great team spirit and friendships. It is also a mini exercise to learn how to manage politics!

The sports also underline the importance of a coach. Even the best players have to be humble and learn from a coach.

So what are you waiting for? Go and search for that ball which is lying somewhere and *'de ghumaake'*!

29

'High Speed Thinking, Low Speed Thinking'!

You are driving your car at 8.30 in the morning on Monday. You have an important meeting where you are expecting many problems. You want to drive fast and reach the office as early as possible. Your mind is racing and the pulse, too! But unfortunately your car isn't. You are caught in a traffic jam! So you start honking more and keep looking for possible gaps in the vehicles to push through. And when you cannot, you explode with frustration. What happened? It was just a mismatch between the speed of your thinking and the speed of the situation. The thinking was high speed but the situation was slow speed.

Our minds have the ability to think at different speeds – just like the gears of a car. When the car is in the first and second gear the driving speed is slow. But the same car can zoom in the fourth and fifth gears when you want to race or overtake other speeding vehicle on the highway. We, too, need to think at different speeds in different situations. It is not just humans, but even the animals have this innate ability to think at different speeds. For example, look at a mother cat when she is feeding her babies. She is all love and calmness and patience. But see the same cat in a fight. It is all high speed thinking and fast actions.

The famous 'fight or flight response' has been acquired by the humans from the animal ancestors. This response was very useful when the ancestors faced dangers in the jungle. Although the humans could think slowly and patiently, they needed a quick response in the face of threats such as a tiger. They had to think quickly and act quickly. When confronted with a danger like this, we can respond in two ways: anger or fear. If we have to attack, the emotion of anger is useful. But if we have to run away, the emotion of fear is useful. Either ways, Adrenaline is secreted in different organs such as the heart to prepare for either flight or fight. This is the 'Adrenaline rush'! Many people know this.

But few people know that a type of Adrenaline is secreted in our brain, too, during the 'flight or fight response'. This literally speeds up the thinking. This high speed thinking is a hallmark of emotional thinking. Observe the speech of persons who are angry of fearful – or even very happy. For example, observe a child who suddenly gets a good news: "Finally, we are going on the vacation!" The child becomes very happy and starts thinking and talking very fast. Or look at a person who is very angry at someone. Again, the speed of thinking and talking is very fast.

High speed thinking is quite useful in certain situations. Consider emergencies such as an accident scene. In such situations, it is very important to think fast and take quick decisions about moving people and objects. Here quick thinking and actions can actually make the difference between life and death. Or consider fast action sports such as basketball. In such sports in addition to reflexive actions, we need quick strategic thinking about where the ball and everyone is, where everyone is headed and what is the best plan of action. Then, there are many exams where we have to solve many questions in a relatively short time where high speed thinking is required.

However, there are many situations where calm and patient thinking is required. A typical example is teaching a young child some new activity such as new game. Observe different parents doing this. Some parents will be calm and unhurried, patiently correcting and encouraging the child. However, some other people cannot stop their high speed thinking. As a result they are impatient, they want quick results from the child. And when they don't get that, the scolding start quickly. This is a typical example of the mismatch between the thinking speed and the situation speed caused by emtions.

In many situations, the mismatch is between thinking speeds of different people. For example, a group of friends suddenly decide to go for a movie. But its only twenty minutes before a movie and they can reach the mall in fifteen minutes. Everyone is ready except one. Now if she says, "I take decisions calmly and unhurriedly. So give me ten minutes to decide". The most likely outcome is that the friends will bang a pillow on her head and leave!

Thus, it is important to observe what your own thinking speed is– in all the different situations. And what is the need of the situation – whether it is a high speed or a low speed situation. If we can adjust the speed of our thinking, the results are nice.

30
TV-like channels of the mind?

The TV is the same. You flick one button and switch on a channel: It's a sad story. Sad faces, lots of crying. Switch on another channel: Everyone is laughing in response to stand-up comedians! Another channel: Anger is boiling like lava! Sharp words lead to bitter fights. Another channel: Everyone is singing and dancing! Switch on a different channel and it is all peace and wisdom and meditation! Remember: the TV is the same. Just change the channel and the atmosphere changes.

Our mind is exactly like this. The mind is the same. But at different times, we can experience all these emotions and thoughts. Suppose you have finished all your chores. Peace reigns at home. You are relaxing, reading a wonderful book. It's the 'Peace channel' going on in your mind. Suddenly, you get a phone call: one of your loved ones has become seriously sick and has been admitted to the hospital. Channel change in your mind: The Thriller channel comes on. It has lots of panic and actions and rushing about. Plenty of sweating and praying, too.

But suppose it is party time. All the buddies have gathered. The Fun - Humour channel gets switched on. You crack jokes, remember jokes and laugh. Where are all the sad stories, the panic – action dramas, the anger and scolding? You do not feel any of those because those channels are not on in your mind. The mind is the same. But as the Emotion channels change everything changes: the topic of thinking, choice of words, future predictions, which memories you remember, whether happy events will give happiness or not (and vice versa) etc. This leads to changes in voice tone, facial expressions, posture and all actions.

For example, consider the Anger channel in the mind. When this channel is on in the mind, you will use harsher words (perhaps swear words), the speed of thinking will be fast (quick retorting), the future predictions will be more negative ("You will suffer...!" etc.). You will remember all bitter memories – and not remember wonderful memories at that time. Happy events will not produce happiness, while unhappy events will trigger more anger. For example, if someone says something nice, it does not make you happy. On the other hand, if someone makes a funny comment, it may induce anger. All these emotions and thinking patterns will lead to changes in facial expressions, voice tone, posture and actions. Even texting becomes fast – and with more typo mistakes! Finally the angry disgust makes you want to avoid people - perhaps humanity!

On the other hand, consider the Love and Kindness channel. When this channel gets switched on in the mind, the words chosen are softer and sweeter. The future predictions are all happy possibilities. All the wonderful memories are remembered, while the unpleasant memories are NOT remembered. You feel like going closer to people. All this pattern of thinking leads to a soft expression on the face, softer voice and a gentler pattern of actions.

With a little observation, you will be able to recognize the features of all the other channels of the mind: the Lazy channel, the Fear channel, the Determination channel, the Pride channel, the Suspicion channel - in addition to all the channels mentioned above! You will be able to recognize the channels in yourself and in others.

What is the use of recognizing these channels in others? Once you recognize what channel is going on the opposite person's mind, you will be able to understand his / her actions better, and will be able to deal with the person better. For example, consider the choice of words. Normally, we interpret words to know what the other person is thinking about a topic. For example, consider the following words: "I wish I had not married you". Should we consider these words as the thoughts of the person – or the thoughts of a particular channel (the Anger channel)? Would the person say the same thing if another channel (e.g. Love channel) was going on in the mind? Understanding this is so vital not only for husband – wife relationship but for every type of relationship.

Recognizing which channel is going on in one's own mind is also useful. Suppose you or others notice that you are making too many negative predictions, try to find out whether it is because of some channel. Then one should work on changing the channel first. Some channels are quite unpleasant. Hence recognizing this becomes the first step in changing the channel in the mind.

How to change the channels in the mind? We don't have a remote for it. But all of us have an innate mental ability to change the channels in the mind. With practice, it can become as easy as saying, "Click"!

31

The opposites of anger and love

Mr. R. And Mrs. P. were once a loving couple. Somehow, due to various stresses, they became irritable and started having angry arguments regularly. As the anger kept on persisting, the love started becoming lesser and lesser. A point came when they seriously considered divorce. A well-wisher suggested marriage counsellor. But they refused, saying, "What will the counsellor tell us that we already do not know?"

No major issues between them and yet they reached the doorstep of divorce. How did it happen?

If you look around, you will find many relationships – not just husband-wife relationships – going through phases of love and anger. How does love bring people together? And, how does anger break relationships?

Problems keep coming all the time. Each problem has many facets to it: What is the extent of problem, what is going to happen, what needs to be done, etc. But there is one aspect of the problem that triggers anger: Who caused the problem? Who is responsible for the problem? It is the blame game that triggers accusations and anger. "Why did the child do poorly in exams? Because of you!" "Why didn't our company get the contract? Because if you!" "Who caused the car accident? You!" And so on.

Anger usually activates the wish for revenge: "You have hurt me, so I will hurt you!" This hurting can be verbal, physical or otherwise – like sabotaging a colleague's chances. The angry person does not feel satisfied till the other person has been 'properly hurt'!

Then a vicious cycle develops. I am angry, so I hurt you. That makes you angry and then you hurt me. And then I retaliate again. And it goes on and on.

It goes on much longer if both want to have the last word. "Why should I back out all the time? Why can't s/he back out?" This feeling is especially stronger if 'the other person having the last word' is considered a Personal Defeat! Nobody likes to be defeated!

Anger has the peculiar property of creating repulsion. If you are really angry with someone, you will detest being with that person! You would like to keep as many kilometres between you and s/he as possible! 'Couples drifting apart' – this is the reason.

Love, on the other hand, creates a force of attraction. Love, here, does not only mean love in a couple, but love in all kinds of relationships: parent-child, siblings, office colleagues, friends – and even love between humans and their pets!

Love creates the feelings of liking, fondness, wishing well, helping, forgiving, etc. But perhaps the main feeling is that of wanting to be close, enjoying the company. This is exactly the opposite of anger. That is why love brings people closer.

Love, too, has its own positive feedback cycle: give love, receive love, give love once again and so on.

What is the use of knowing all this info about anger and love? We keep finding ourselves or people known to us in angry relationships. That is the time to put this knowledge to use. The most important thing is to turn off anger. Anger is rarely without some justification. So you have a reason and right to be angry. But if you let go off your right to be angry and the right to hit back, you will be rewarded with a better, happier and long-lasting relationship.

You cannot fight fire with fire. But you can fight fire with ice. Undoubtedly, it is easier said than done. But if you can swallow your anger, you will be able to enjoy a pleasing relationship. People who are able to control their anger, have much better relationships at home, at workplace and with friends.

But turning off the anger is only half of the story. The second thing to do is to turn on the love. This is very difficult when you have gone through an angry phase and you have boiling resentment inside you. Take your time to cool down and then try again.

What frequently happens is that one person cools down but the other person is still sharpening knives inside the mind! One person offers the hand of friendship, but the other person spits fire. The first person, who has barely controlled his/her anger, promptly concludes, "See! It is not going to work out. I have tried. I have given it a chance. But, see! S/he is not interested. So the thing is not going to work out." Such complexities! If both persist with more love and less anger, things can really improve.

Turning on love does not necessarily mean saying coochi coochi words! Simple, nice, friendly words and actions can attract people.

Be angry and the people will go away from you! Or be loving and nice and people will be attracted to you!

32
Why people become emotional

All of us know people who are 'emotional'. Some people are prone to anger: they become angry often – and quite intensely. Then there are people who are always sad. Slightest problem and they start crying. There are some who are extremely anxious. They are afraid of many things. Slightest hint of trouble and they start imagining the worst. Then, of course, we know people who are 'happiness-prone'! They are always cheerful, they laugh easily and keep seeing the humorous angle of every situation.

Why is it that different people are emotional for different emotions i.e. prone to different emotions. Some people are prone to two or more emotions. For example, we know people who are generally cheerful but when they become angry, they just blow up!

It is also true that this 'emotionality' or 'emotion-proneness' can change over time. We all know people who were once cheerful but due to some reasons, have become sadness-prone or fearful or irritable.

This article describes the reasons why different people become emotional i.e. prone to different emotions. What is it that determines the intensity of emotions. When different people are exposed similar situations or problems, they show different emotional reactions. For example, when you hear the news that a close relative has been admitted to a hospital. Do you react with intense fear or sadness or anger (related to somebody's carelessness etc.)? Or you become disturbed a little but regain calmness immediately? What is it that determines the intensity of the emotions?

One of the main factors that determines the intensity of emotions is the intensity of the wish involved. For example, if a student has an intense wish to win a competition, then the resulting emotion will be intense. If the student wins, he will be very happy. But if s/he loses then s/he will be very sad. On the other hand, if the wish is not intense, the emotions will be less intense.

The degree of wish fulfilment, too, determines the intensity of emotions. For example, if a sportsperson wins the gold medal, s/he will be very happy. If s/he wins the silver or bronze, s/he will be less happy. Of course, if the sportsperson was sure of winning the gold, s/he may actually become very, very unhappy if s/he wins the silver medal!

The pre-existing mood, too, determines the intensity of emotions. For example, suppose, you are not afraid of the dark. But you see a horror movie at night. So, you get into a fearful mood. Then you get into bed to sleep. At that time, suddenly you hear a noise outside your house. You are likely to be startled – which normally you would not. This is the impact of the pre-existing mood. This is true for all emotions. Suppose, you have watched some 'angry' movie or TV programme or speech. Then if you see or read about some 'injustice' you are likely to react with more intense anger than you normally would. This is how different leaders or movies use media to incite different emotions in a large number of people.

One peculiar property of the emotions is that when a particular emotion becomes too intense, it can inhibit other emotions.

For example, sometimes we experience a mixture of emotions. Consider a roller-coaster ride. We experience a mixture of happiness and fear. But suppose, on a particular ride we get the belief that the roller-coaster is about to break. Then, suddenly, fear will become intense. It will suppress the happiness completely. This type of suppression of one emotion by another can be seen with all emotions. If a person is intensely sad and depressed, that sadness will supress the happiness completely. Even if such a person is offered some food that s/he normally loves, s/he will not experience any happiness.

This is reverse emotionality. The person cannot experience an emotion because it has been suppressed by another more intense emotion.

The most important property of Emotion Centres is that if a particular Emotion Centre is used often, it becomes more excitable. This means the person becomes more prone to that emotion. Suppose a person becomes angry repeatedly. Then her/his Anger Centre will become more excitable: s/he will become prone to that emotion. This emotion-proneness means a small anger provoking incident will trigger a much more intense anger. The same is true for other emotions, too. If a person becomes afraid often, s/he will become prone to fear. The same for sadness and happiness.

As can be seen, this becomes a self-perpetuating process. Because you became sad often, you become prone to sadness. This in turn leads to more sadness.

We can use this knowledge to our advantage. We can choose to become happiness-prone and less prone to sadness, fear and anger!

33
The 'Thought Replay System' of the mind

Mr. T.P. has a fear of road accidents. Because of that, any time a family member or friend goes on a road journey, TP becomes obsessed with the fearful thoughts. He constantly keeps thinking of only one thought: Is s/he safe? If the journey is to last for six hours, for those six hours he will able to do nothing except think of the traveller. He might call up that person every half an hour just to check if all is well. He is not be able to work or even enjoy a movie. Even if he tries to concentrate on some work, his mind keeps replaying the same fearful thoughts and he gives up the work to continue the fearful line of thinking again. This is the mind's Thought Replay System in action!

Our minds have this peculiar system. The system spontaneously replays the important thoughts again and again. You must have noticed this: Suppose you have had some intensely emotional thoughts - such as some highly emotion-charged arguments with someone. Later you decide to 'forget it and get on with the work'. Yet, you find that those unpleasant, unwanted thoughts keep coming back to mind and prevent you from concentrating on the work at hand. Sometimes even the happy emotional thoughts (such as India winning the World Cup) keep coming back into the mind – in spite of our wanting to avoid thinking about them (in order to concentrate on the work).

This is the Thought Replay System. This is just like the Action Replay we see in the matches. For example, in cricket matches, if a batsman hits a six, it is replayed a few times as the Action Replay. Our minds have an autonomous system for the same function – the Thought Replay System (TRS).

Observe this: You read many news items in the newspaper in the morning. Then, many times during the day, you will remember some of the news items. 'Your thoughts keep going back to those news items'. This is the TRS doing its job! But you do not remember all the news items – only some of them. So, which ones do you remember - and which ones you don't? Those news items which elicited a lot of emotions (happy or unhappy), are picked up by the TRS and replayed later. For example, if some political news made you emotional (happy or unhappy), that topic will be replayed by the Thought Replay System.

This system is autonomous i.e. it is not under our direct voluntary control. This means even if we want to stop the replay of thoughts, we cannot do it immediately. For example, suppose a person is suffering from intense sad thoughts related to the death of a loved one. The person is unable to 'shake it off' i.e. unable to stop the replay of the painful thoughts by the TRS. In fact, such unpleasant or painful replay of thoughts troubles many people who are suffering from disorders such as Obsessive Compulsive

Disorder (OCD), Post Traumatic Stress Disorder (PTSD), Depression and Anxiety disorders. Some of the people suffering from OCD, have an irrational fear of germs present on the hands. So, they wash their hands extra thoroughly with lots of soap and water. An average person would then forget the germs on the hand and get on with other work. But even if the person with OCD tries to do so, the thoughts about the possibility of germs remaining on the hand continue to be replayed – again and again. The fear then pushes the person to wash the hands again. In some people, this goes on fifteen, twenty or even more number of times. Even if the person tries to distract himself/herself, the thoughts are replayed again.

In such cases or in the case of Mr. T.P., why does the replay continue many times? There is a vicious cycle happening in the mind. The Thought Replay System replays the emotional thoughts. But after such thoughts have been replayed and the person is thinking about the topic emotionally. Then, this emotional thinking becomes a source for the TRS, and the TRS replays the thought yet again. Thus. this vicious cycle continues – till the person is able to distract herself/himself.

So many of us are unable to 'switch off' the office thoughts after going home – even if we want to. Now you know the reason: the Thought Replay System!

Does all this mean that the Thought Replay System of the mind is only a troublesome system? Oh, no! It is quite a useful system, too. The Thought Replay makes us come 'back on track' despite disturbances. For example, suppose you are doing some work. You suddenly hear a loud noise and some commotion on the street outside. So, naturally, you go and see what is happening. You become engrossed in the scene outside. But after some time, 'suddenly you remember' what work you were doing and you come back to continue the work. This was the Thought Replay System in action! It reminded you of the important work you were doing earlier - by replaying the thoughts about it. Thus the TRS helps us to resume our work in spite of distractions in between.

When the Thought Replay is of happy thoughts, we like it. This happy replay reminds us again and again of the happy events (such some good news about a loved one or winning a prize etc.). This happy replay keeps giving us a lot of satisfaction for a long, long time. Sometimes the happy thoughts could be an enjoyable song or a tune. You must have noticed this: you hear some song in the morning. And then, many times during the day, you find yourself remembering and humming that song– without you actually wishing to remember it. It automatically 'comes to your mind'.

How to stop the replay of unpleasant, unwanted thoughts? The first thing is realizing that "I am not thinking about it again and again', but rather 'the TRS is replaying the thoughts – against my wishes'. Then, one can consciously eliminate that unpleasant line of thought – as soon as it is replayed. The best method is to deliberately focus the attention on some other topic with full attention. This may have to be done many times to counter the repeated replay. Eventually, the thought replay stops.

Thus the Thought Replay System is a useful system. But if starts replaying unpleasant, unwanted thoughts, then it needs to countered.

34

Short Term Happiness versus Long Term Happiness

"Should I go for the movie along with my friends or should I study for the forthcoming exam?" "Should I spend money on that expensive dress or should I save?" "Should I have that peg or should I prefer a sickness-free life?"

These are dilemmas that all of us face every day. Sometimes one option seems better and sometimes the other. In the end, what is right for me: should I have that delicious but high fat dish or I should think of my goal of reducing my weight? How should I decide what I should do? If we understand the dynamics involved, we can choose better. In all such decisions the choice is between Short Term Happiness versus Long Term Happiness.

We all want to be happy – now and forever! So, naturally, what all of us want is enjoying all the things that give us S.T. Happiness and L.T. Happiness. What we would like to do is enjoying huge quantities of tasty, fatty foods – and yet remain slim and fit! But the life is not so easy. We have to choose between such two options so many times. If we enjoy the S.T. Happiness, we have to give up the L.T. Happiness. And vice versa.

For example, would you cut short your beauty sleep by half an hour to go for the morning walk? Sleeping for that half hour is a typical S.T. Happiness. But resisting the pull of the comfy bed and putting on the jogging shoes is going to give L.T. Happiness – the joy of feeling fit throughout the day and throughout the life. Here, the important trick is to realize that the morning walk is not a bitter pill with unseen long term benefits. If we have a positive attitude, we can actually enjoy the morning walks. The pleasant weather, the quiet roads and the sight of like-minded fitness enthusiasts doing their walking and exercising happily. Once we start enjoying the morning walks, they become a source of Short Term Happiness, too!

If we start loving the activities that are for L.T. Happiness, they start giving us S.T. Happiness, too.

But there are some activities that give S.T. Happiness but actually give L.T. Unhappiness. Consider addictions such as smoking or drinking. They are tricky because they don't produce side-effects initially. But over the years, they start producing various health problems – small and major – even life-threatening. For example, consider a person who drinks regularly. For some years there are no side-effects. So for this person, alcohol is a source of S.T. Happiness – and with no unhappiness. Later the liver gives in. The person gets cirrhosis and is admitted to hospital with blood vomits. The person now faces a life of deteriorating health and repeated hospitalizations for treatment of various sicknesses. The person's dear ones, too, suffer – seeing the suffering, financial burden and because of the need to give chronic nursing care.

What was once a distant, unseen L.T. Unhappiness, finally arrives in the house like a permanent, unwanted guest. At this stage, it is not easy for the person to say, "I have enjoyed a lot, and now it is okay for me and my dear ones to suffer for the years to come." What was once an easy trade-off - "I will enjoy for years, *baaki ek din toh sabko marna hai.*" – no longer seems worthwhile. Short Term Happiness with Long Term Unhappiness versus Long Term Happiness: what will you choose?

The apparent trick is to enjoy S.T. Happiness in moderation so as to avoid L.T. Unhappiness. For example, consider an overweight person. One such person came to me wishing for weight loss. He asked me the diet to be followed. I started off: "Avoid oily, fried, sweets ..." He interrupted me and said, "Why bother telling me all the long list. Why don't you just tell me to stop eating everything that I like!" The smart people enjoy small portions of all such foods and get to enjoy the taste. And by eating small portions, they manage to keep obesity away.

Are achievments a type of S.T. Happiness or L.T. Happiness? For example, a person works hard and wins a sports medal. Is it just a S.T. Happy event or a source of L.T. Happiness? An important ingredient in Long Term Happiness is the feeling of 'satisfaction'. If we count our blessing and achievements with a long-lasting satisfaction, we can get Long Term Happiness. If we quickly forget them and get back to counting what we haven't got, they become a source of only Short Term Happiness.

And so, that's the story of Short Term Happiness versus Long Term Happiness. Decide how you are going to solve your own dilemmas while I solve mine: "What size piece of this cake will give me Short Term Happiness – while ensuring Long Term Happiness!"

35
How self-fulfilling predictions come true

A three years old child develops a simple cold, cough. So he is taken to the doctor for a check-up. On the way, the child starts making predictions in his mind about how horrible the ordeal of the check-up is going to be. Tension starts building up in his mind as they reach the clinic. By the time his turn comes and parents take him inside the cabin, his tension has reached peak. When, finally, he is made to lie down on the examination bed, all hell breaks loose! With a torch in hand, the doctor asks him to open his mouth. The response from child is an 80 decibel vehement bawling "No"! A lot of coaxing by the doctor and parents has no impact. Finally, the doctor asks the parents to hold the child tight. Then the doc pushes a tongue depressor into the mouth. The child shakes his head with all his might. At last, the impossible looking task of examining the child's throat is over. But, for the child, his prediction has come true: the check-up by the doctor is indeed a terrible experience!

Another three years old has to undergo exactly the same check-up. Her prophecy is exactly the opposite: the doc is a nice person and the check-up is a pleasant experience. So, she happily climbs on the examination table and when the doc says, "Open your mouth", she does it happily. The result: No struggling, no crying, no thrusting tongue depressor into mouth, check-up over in seconds and "Good girl!" from everyone. Importantly: her prophecy has also come true!

Both were 'Self-fulfilling predictions'. Each child made a certain mental prediction which ultimately turned out to be true. Even if each child had made the other prediction, it would still have come true. Is it magic? How does it work out?

We keep making mental predictions all the time: 'My meeting with the boss is going to turn out bad', 'I am going to get jitters on stage while making the presentation', 'I am going to enjoy the party' and so on. The predictions can be negative or positive. So, how do they turn out to be true?

Consider negative predictions. For example, consider a boxer in the ring who has got ready to hit out – hands in boxing position, footwork starts and most importantly, adrenaline start flowing. Slightest move by the opponent and the boxer quickly hits out.

Our verbal duels are quite similar. You make a mental prediction that your meeting with the colleagues is going to be an unpleasant and irritating experience. Now, let us see how this becomes a self-fulfilling prophecy. You anticipate insult and injustice and verbal fights. So even before the meeting, you get into a 'fighting mode' - ready to 'fight it out'. Your adrenaline is flowing and you are looking for the first signs of trouble – ready to pounce upon your opponents! Somebody makes a slightly unpleasant remark and you say to yourself, 'Here it starts'. So you attack. Naturally, the verbal fight ensues. So, you tell yourself, 'See, my prediction has come true: it was an unpleasant experience.'

Every day, every week, we can find astrological predictions in the newspapers and magazines that are based on zodiac signs. Imagine: this prediction is going to turn out to be true for one-twelfth of the world population - approximately 616 million people! Yet, many people say it does come true. Magic?

One peculiar aspect of this type of predictions is that, first, we make a hypothesis: how the situation is going to turn out. And so, we start looking for the signs – selectively. For example, if the prediction says, 'you will have health problems in the next week', you start looking for signs of health problems. Slightest acidity, and you say the prediction has come true!

This type of 'mental filtering' becomes very important in relationships. If you make a hypothesis that 'this person is nice', then you start looking for signs of niceness in her or him. It your hypothesis is that the person is nasty, you start looking for signs of nastiness. As the reality is, most of the people have a combination of these two. So both predictions turn out to be true.

This is not only true for people but for situations, too. For example, parents want children to meet different relatives or friends. How the situation turns out, can depend on the prediction that the children make: happy or sad or frightening or irritating or, most commonly, BORING!

As you keep making your predictions (happy and unhappy) through the day, observe these points: By making that prediction, are your efforts changing? Are you selectively filtering your observations? Are you colouring people or situations? Then you will understand the magic of 'Self-fulfilling prophecies'!

36
Are you ready to face your next problem?

Every single person in the world has problems – either of this type or that type.

And this is true for every person who has lived! Did you think that only you have problems – and 'others' don't have problems? Then, this will come as a surprise. But you must be thinking: How come 'they' always look happy and satisfied and smart, while you feel so unhappy on the inside? The big news is this: it does not mean that 'they' do not have problems, but that they have learnt to adapt and adjust to the problems, to be comfortable in spite of the problems, to put the problems in a corner of the mind and not allow the problems to dominate the mind.

Can everyone learn this trick? Can you learn how to take the problems in the stride and be at ease even in the middle of the problems? Yes, you can also learn how to do this. It is said, – in a funny but true way – that the trouble with learning from experience is that you get the exams before the tuitions! How to learn facing the problems – while we are already in battle with them? But it can be done.

All of us get two categories of problems: (1) "The bolt from the blue" kind of problem. Such problems are sudden and unexpected. But they are rare. (2) "The again and again" kind of problems. Most of our day to day problems belong to this category. Everyone, typically has five or six problems that keep coming back again and again. For example, office pressures or interpersonal problems at home, office or in social circles. Most such problems are related to frictions of different types of personalities. If personalities will not change, such frictions will keep creating problems. For example, consider different viewpoints between husband and wife or between parents and children or between in-laws. Or consider interpersonal problems in the office. Such problems typically keep bothering again and again and yet again. The majority of our problems are of this type.

One way of looking at it, is to think, "Oh, no! This problems is likely to trouble me again and again." The other way of looking at it is, "If I know such as a problem is going to come – in advance – then I can be ready for it, ready to tackle it in a much better way. By knowing that a particular problem is going to come, I get a chance to prepare myself for it." And this 'anticipatory preparedness' is what this article is about.

By anticipating and by preparing for the problems, we can tackle them in a much better way. The best time to prepare is when there is free time, when you are not in an emotional turmoil already. The first step in this is to write down and make a list of all the problems. Writing is such a useful activity. It helps to crystallize our thoughts, so that we can understand the problem much better. For example, K.P., an employee of a company had some unpleasant experiences in his office. Gradually, he came to detest going to the office. But he could not exactly explain why he was unhappy about the office. He said it was the atmosphere in the office. When probed further, he said, it was office politics. When I suggested him to write down his problems, his thoughts started becoming clearer. It was the unhealthy competition between him and some other colleagues that was actually encouraged by a crafty boss. The boss would constantly praise his colleagues (and competitors for the promotion), while demeaning him - apparently to prod him to give better performance in sales.

When he started writing down the problem, the picture became clear. Now it became easy for him to know what to do. Could he change the boss's brain? No. Could he leave the company? No. But he could see through the boss's gameplan and mentally be ready for it. K.P. was basically a smart person. So he decided beforehand and mentally prepared himself for the boss's next needling. He told me later that by understanding his boss's personality and by being ready for it, he can now keep his cool when meeting the boss.

This is being ready for the next problem! If the problem is a recurring problem, then either we can dread the problem, or we can mentally be ready for the challenge. Many of the domestic problems are of the recurring type. For example, teenager's tantrums and parents' shoutings. Anger leads to revenge leads to more anger leads to more revenge and so on! Preparing mentally beforehand can help to minimize such problems. For example, suppose a parent realizes that s/he is overreacting to the child's tantrums. When the parent is alone and calm, s/he can decide and practise a better emotional response – as compared to the typical angry outburst. Such mental visualization and rehearsal helps a lot to give a better performance when the situation arises. "I will be cool, I will be cool – even if the child is throwing his/her typical tantrum!"

All of us are smart enough to know what is the best or most appropriate response to any situation. But if we are going decide what to do at the spur of the moment, in the middle of the turmoil, then we may not give our best. This is where anticipatory preparation helps.

If we are able to control our reactions, generally the result of the interaction is better. The outcome is better. But even if the outcome is not as good as we wanted, we can remain more cool and calm as a result of the mental preparation.

So if you want to solve or at least minimize your problems, take charge. Begin by writing down your typical five or six problems. Identify what the problem areas are. And then mentally rehearse and prepare yourself – to give your performance!

37
Feeling lonely in the midst of people?

Mrs. N. S. is a forty eight years-old mother of two teenagers living with her husband. Her father passed away two years ago. And her mother died six months ago. She was feeling depressed after her father's death. But after her mother's death, she started feeling very lonely. This was in spite of her actively living with her own family. It was very difficult for her husband or kids to understand how she can feel alone when they are with her.

There are many people who feel quite lonely even if living in the midst of people. Nowadays, so many people migrate – from their village to a faraway city, or from own country to another. There are two kinds of people – extroverts and introverts. Extroverts are talkative, friendly. They love mixing with people and making new friends. The introverts are not so talkative and they are not very good at making new friends. When they migrate, the extroverts make friends quickly. So they don't remain alone for a long time. On the other hand, when introverts migrate, they are at a risk of being lonely. We can see many such who are working in the office whole day surrounded by people. Yet they continue to feel lonely at heart. Although they indulge in work talk and small talk, they miss the heart to heart talk.

In order to feel connected, we humans need heart to heart talk in which we can share our emotional feelings – sad or happy. It is a wonderful fact of life that if we share our happiness, it increases. And if we share unhappiness, it reduces. For example, suppose you are seeing a cricket match – and India is winning. Now, what will give you more happiness – watching the match alone or watching with a bunch of friends? Obviously, when you are sharing the joy with the cheering friends, isn't it?

Now, consider the opposite situation: you are feeling miserable because of some unhappy situation. If you have a sympathetic relative or friend, you will feel much lighter after sharing your problems with the person. If you don't have such a good person, you will continue to languish in the misery for a long time – and feel very, very lonely. 'Water, water everywhere but not drop to drink'! Lots of people all around, but not a friend to share!

But, sometimes, a person can feel lonely in spite of having good people around – because of depression. If a person is depressed, the attitude towards others changes. Love brings people closer, but depression and irritability makes a person detached or disgusted about others. It makes you feel like avoiding others: exactly the opposite of opening one's heart out. The same person, in a happier mood will not find others so dislikeable. So, if you are feeling very lonely, first check whether the people around are not nice or whether it is your mood that is making you feel detached.

When a person starts feeling lonely, many problems start. The first and foremost is brooding. The same thoughts keep coming to the mind again and again and again. This is like blowing air into a balloon again and again. The balloon begins to appear bigger and bigger. In the same way, any unhappy thought becomes more and more intense. One starts feeling that the problem is very big – when actually it is not. For example, an employee was scolded by the boss for some delayed work. The boss said that the employee may also lose her job. After this she went into a brooding mode: how the boss 'insulted' her and what will happen if she loses her job. Feeling lonely, she continued to brood, not sharing it woth anyone. The balloon in her mind started becoming bigger an bigger – leading to more and more miserable feeling. Finally, one day she talked to a sympathetic colleague. He immediately corrected her misconceptions by telling how this is the normal scolding by the boss and how the job loss threat is not to be taken seriously. Brooding - misery, sharing – relief.

Man is a social animal. We need to talk to many people – in the same way that we need to eat a variety of foods to remain healthy. Social withdrawal (not feeling like talking to anyone), magnifies many mental problems. This can then lead to the intensity of mental disorders.

Nowadays, with the advent of so many communication avenues such as the mobile and the social media, it is so easy to connect and be in touch with relatives and friends. So, even migrants need not feel lonely.

People who have not felt lonely, find it very difficult to understand how a person can feel lonely in the midst of people. But if you indeed find a lonely person please go ahead and connect. It means a lot to him or her.

38
How the environment shapes the mind

Observe yourself: when you pick up your newspaper to read, which pages do you read first? Front page? Financial or stock market? International? Sports page? Or some other page?

Or observe yourself: When you open the whatsapp, which chat do you read first? Which groups'? Which friends'?

Reading the newspaper or reading the whatsapp are exclusively personal actions. Nobody tells us what to read first. Yet, we have developed certain preferences over time. How do these preferences develop? Are these preferences created in our mind by the people or the environment we live in?

Everyone knows that the environment influences our minds. But exactly how does it influence? Here 'environment' does not mean only the weather, but mainly the people we come across or the ideas we come across. They may be people we actually meet. Or the people we come across through media: books, TV, internet or social media such as Facebook or Whatsapp. Sometimes, we don't even know whose ideas we are receiving. For example, most of the times, we do not know the people who have created the advertisements. Yet these people or their ideas influence our minds.

The most important point to be noted is this: 'Environment shapes our minds, but we choose our environment'! We choose whom we spend our time with. For example, on weekends, whom are you going to spend your time with? Who are your 'friends' or 'peers'? How do we choose our friends or peers or groups?

'Birds of a feather flock together' is half of the story! People who have a common liking come together. For example, if you have some religious interest, you choose religious people as your peers. So, you may join some religious group. Or if you have a liking for nature, you may join a nature group. And so on for other wishes such as drinking alcohol, social service, professional interests etc.

But what happens after we join a group – or develop friendship with like-minded people? That is the other half of the story! Initially, you may have a mild or moderate level interest. But when you spend more time with those people, your beliefs and wishes become stronger and more intense. That topic starts becoming more important in your life. This is true for all the different interests that all such groups have. For example, the interests may as varied as the following: saving the animals, traveling, taking 'weed' or other drugs, hating and doing mass killings of people of other religions, enjoying literature, trekking, various nerdy activities (such as writing software), helping needy people etc.

In all such groups, there are 'leaders' who themselves are highly motivated. This means they have intense beliefs and wishes. And they are willing to put in efforts to fulfil the wishes. One basic desire of all human beings is to spread one's own beliefs and wishes. And in the process, convert other people to one's ideology. This is true for all the spheres of human activity – such as those mentioned above. If you find something good, you motivate others to try it. It may mean recommending a restaurant or a religious guru or a political party or a brand of alcohol and so on. All of us want others to do the activities that we find good or important. So we try to 'sell' our ideas to others! We strive to create more followers or peers.

So, when we join such groups, the beliefs and wishes become more intense and we become more and more motivated to those activities. So, you start spending even more time with group doing those activities!

One important aspect of such an effect is that we mould ourselves (change our behaviour) to fit into the group, to be accepted by the group members. If you join a nature group, this may translate into giving up plastic bags. If you join a gangster group, this may mean speaking foul language and becoming aggressive. If you join a drinkers group, this may mean praising and glorifying alcohol. And so on.

Advertising is an important part of our environment. Advertisers want a place in your mind. All advertisements want to create specific beliefs in your mind. For example, this brand of deo will attract ladies to you! That brand of TV has the best picture quality. (Never mind that the 'excellent picture quality' that you are seeing in that advertisement – you are actually seeing on your good old TV!)

When we develop such beliefs, it translates into wishes – wishes to buy those products. When the wish becomes sufficiently intense, it translates into the advertisers' dream: we spend cash on that brand!

It useful to understand how the environment, the people influence our mind – our beliefs, wishes and behaviour.

39
The magic potion called Enthusiasm

A group of college friends is sitting and chatting. With nothing specific to do, the atmosphere is slowly getting boring. People start talking about how it is getting late and how there is study and work to be done. Then suddenly one enthusiastic person gets a brainwave, "Let us play our old game ..." And suddenly the atmosphere changes. Everyone shouts, "Yesss! Let's play!!" Everyone gets up and starts talking animatedly. Suddenly no one is bored. Everyone is already feeling happy – even before the game has begun. How did it happen? Yes! They have taken the magic potion called Enthusiasm!

What, exactly, happened in the minds of all these guys when Enthusiasm arrived? How does the Enthusiasm perform its magic?

There are many types of happiness: peace, calmness, smile, satisfaction, relief, pleasure etc. But Enthusiasm is a very special type of happiness. There are many facets in the wonderful thing called Enthusiasm.

We experience most types of happiness when something good has happened. For example, we get the pleasure of eating a particular food *after* we have eaten it. But the main ingredient in the feeling of enthusiasm is anticipatory happiness. In the example of the friends described above, everyone suddenly started expecting fun and enjoyment from the game they decided to play. And that is what made them happy. All of us know the joy we experience when we are leaving for a vacation. We feel happy even before the vacation has begun!

However, it is not that we feel happy about getting some happiness at the end of the journey When Enthusiasm arrives, the whole journey becomes enjoyable. Enthusiasm is that magic potion which transforms how we think in many ways. For example, enthusiasm simply increases the happiness level and thereby changes our decision making. Consider the simple decision about accepting the responsibility of arranging some games for the children. If you are feeling a little tired or bored, you might decide in favour of not taking up the responsibility. The bother of making the arrangements seems more than the expected enjoyment. However if you are enthusiastic, you will happily put in all the efforts required to make the games successful. The net result: games that everyone enjoyed thoroughly! If you were not enthusiastic, the result would have been 'no games'.

The prime effect Enthusiasm has on people is that they become active. When we are arranging a party enthusiastically, we are able to work much harder than what we would expect. We happily stay up late or get up early – and feel happy about it! We can also work faster if we are enthusiastic. You must have noticed that when enthusiastic, people actually walk faster and even talk faster! When Enthusiasm comes, adrenaline flows – but not out of fear but because of happiness. You feel all charged up!

One other effect of the enthusiastic mood is that we are able to manage and get over small irritants more easily. Suppose, there is some event in the office. Everyone is enthusiastic about it. Undoubtedly, there will be small glitches and petty politics. But if everyone is enthusiastic, then such small problems get smoothened out easily and quickly. And everyone gets back into enthu mood again. If there is one leadership quality that is more important than all others, it is 'Enthusiasm'!

All moods are infectious: sad mood, angry or irritable mood – and even enthusiastic mood. For example, you are calm. But you meet a person who is in an irritated mood. It is quite possible that in the next few minutes you will become irritated, too. The same thing is true for the enthu mood. You must be knowing some enthu persons who can change the atmosphere in a room when they arrive. When such enthusiastic people talk and work, everyone suddenly starts feeling happy and optimistic. This is what a great leader can achieve. S/he may be the leader of a social group or a marketing department or a company. If s/he can inject enthusiasm into people, the group becomes not only happy but productive, too.

One of the major effects of enthusiasm is that it produces optimism. Hope is inbuilt in the emotion of Enthusiasm. And enthusiasm not only produces hope, it gives the energy to achieve success. You must have observed this. A sports team is discussing a forthcoming tough match: the opponents are known to be better and defeat seems quite likely. And so, everyone is in a gloomy mood. But it so happens that the coach or captain or even a member of the team is able to generate enthusiasm. Soon everyone gets into the enthu mood. In the gloomy mood, people might be talking about how the other team is better in so many aspects. But in the enthu mood, people start talking about their own team's abilities. "Come on! Let's fight!" So, finally, with this battle cry, the team members decide to give it their best shot – whether they win or lose! And we all have seen such enthu charged teams go on to win against better opponents.

We can learn several things from this. The first is that the opposite of enthusiasm is gloom and depression – and even boredom! The thinking and the actions that result from a gloomy mood are quite the opposite of what we get in an enthusiastic mood. So, suppose you have some work in front of you but you are in a gloomy, pessimistic mood. Rather than forcing yourself while in the gloomy mood, it is worthwhile changing the mood to enthu first.

That is the second thing to be learned: it is possible for everyone to consciously and deliberately change the mood from dull, bored or depressed - to the Enthu mood. We humans have this innate mental ability to control our emotions. We can either activate or inactivate our emotions. For example, if are very angry, you can tell yourself, "Cool down, cool down". And soon your anger comes down and you become cool again. In the same way, we can charge up our enthusiasm. "COME ON! LET'S GET GOING!"

So what are you waiting for? Drink up your magic potion of Enthusiasm AND GET GOING!

40
The Blame Game

"Yeh sab tumhare laad pyaar ka natija hai!" ("Our son/ daughter has got spoilt because of your pampering!") So shouts the typical father at the typical mother in the typical hindi movie! Finding someone to blame for any problem is a favourite pastime for all of us. There is this joke. An irate husband complains to the in-laws about his wife: "Your product has a manufacturing defect. Please replace!" The in-laws reply: "The product is more than eighteen years old. Manufacturer's liability is over. It is now the user's responsibility!"

A few times like this, the blaming can be funny. But more often, it generates a lot of bitterness – and politics! If we understand the dynamics of the Blame Game, we can avoid the bitterness and turn it into a productive exercise.

The Blame Game keeps happening everywhere, all the time: at home, in the office, in social groups (such as building societies) etc. But the undisputable masters are the politicians who love to blame the opposite parties for personal gains.

This game begins with a problem – any problem. The problem may be as simple as the child forgetting to take a notebook to school or it may be as big as the country's team losing in a match. The essential first step in the Blame Game is to consider the problem as a 'mistake'. Obviously, if it is a mistake, it has to be somebody's mistake!

One key feature of human intelligence is the ability to identify causes of events – and problems. If we get a stomach upset, immediately we think, "What did I eat yesterday?" If a company starts making losses, everyone starts thinking, "Why?" When a neighbour's family ends in a divorce, everyone goes into overdrive thinking about the causes.

The most important point to understand is this: was the problem caused by the mistake of a human or was it the result of unfortunate circumstances? And even if it was the mistake of a person, was it an unintentional mistake or was it a deliberate harm? This analysis decides what will be the outcome of the game.

There are two categories of people as far as this topic is concerned. One category is the group of Blamers and the other category is the Problem Solvers. These two persons have quite different attitudes towards the topic of 'problems'. And hence they take the issue to totally opposite directions.

The Blamer is always convinced that every problem is hundred percent the result of somebody's mistake. Hence they believe that ALL problems are ALWAYS avoidable! They refuse to believe that problems can happen because of unfortunate circumstances. For example, if some family member becomes sick, the Blamer is absolutely sure that the sickness happened because of someone's mistake. So this person's analysis does not go in the direction of what caused it, but rather who has caused it. So the Blamer thinks, "The patient must have done something wrong or must not have taken care or forgotten to take medicines or some such mistake."

The Blamer then feels it necessary to publicly put the blame on that person – with lots of harsh words. "You are so incompetent, careless, insensitive. If you were more careful, this problem would not have occurred. You are responsible for all the sufferings of all the people." And so on. For the Blamer, punishing the guilty is far more important than solving / preventing problems. The Blamer naively believes that if you publicly scold or humiliate or punish the guilty person, s/he will feel truly guilty and will fall on knees begging for forgiveness and repent! Actually, in the real world, in case or real people, nothing like this happens! If you publicly humiliate a person, the person becomes very angry. And like every angry person, s/he seeks revenge. The person then retaliates – either by shifting the blame back on to the Blamer or by remembering some mistake that the Blamer had made earlier. This naturally makes the Blamer more angry. And so the duel begins!

Most importantly, this exercise, which began as a 'cause-finding and problem-solving exercise', goes in a totally unpleasant and counterproductive direction. One encounters such Blamers everywhere: at home, in the office, in social groups (including whatsapp groups!) and in government / politics.

On the hand, the Problem Solvers have a totally different attitude. They never lose sight of the basic aim: to solve the problem or to ensure that the problem does not occur again! They understand that every problem is not necessarily caused by somebody's mistake. Problems can happen because of unfortunate circumstances, too. So, they don't rush into a CID or Police mode when they encounter a problem. They don't adopt the roles of police or judges. They remain administrators whose job is to ensure smooth functioning – of home or office.

But, suppose the problem is really caused be someone's mistake. Then how does the Problem Solver respond? Suppose there is some function – at home or in the office. One person has been given the job of purchasing the gifts to be given. And the person forgets. Or, suppose there some fault in the computer and the job of calling the mechanic has been entrusted to someone. And s/he forgets. How does the Problem Solver respond? Undoubtedly, sometimes scolding has to be done. The Problem Solver prefers to do it in private and not publicly – to avoid unnecessary humiliation of an otherwise good person. But sometimes, the scolding has to be done publicly – so that everyone learns the lesson. The Problem Solver does it proactively – with a genuine aim of preventing problems in future. And not as a means releasing pent up frustrations.

One typical human tendency is to avoid the blame by passing it on to someone else. If the blaming and scolding is harsh, there is more tendency of passing the buck. If the cause –finding is genuine, people are more likely to take the responsibility for their mistakes.

Take the case of the recent train accident. What did the sensationalist television channels shout as their headlines: "Who is responsible?" None of the media discussed what specific steps need to be taken to prevent such accidents in future.

The Blamers or the Problem Solvers – which group do you belong to?

41
The secret of creativity

Walt Disney observed a mouse running about, added a dash of human characteristics and, in the process, created the fabulously popular Mickey Mouse! The Earl of Sandwich told his cook to create a novel dish. The result: the timelessly loved recipe called sandwich! J. K Rowling created unforgettable characters and mixed them with a magical wand to create the stupendously adored Harry Potter series. Edison did not discover any laws of physics nor any new elements. But he used known metals and known physics laws to create the revolutionary electric bulb!

The magic of creativity wows us. Whenever we see a marvellous designed building, we feel like saluting the architect and engineer who created the wonderful design. What, exactly, is creativity? Many people, including some of the creative artistes, say that creativity is a natural, inborn or god-given talent. But can we study and understand creativity? And, most importantly, can we learn to be creative? The answer is yes. That, in fact, is the aim of this article.

Creativity basically means creating a new pattern from previously known units or parts. There's this old story. A friend accused an author of plagiarism. The author was furious. The friend said, with a twinkle in his eye, "Every word that you have written is from a book that I have." The author demanded to see the book. The friend burst out laughing and said, "It is the dictionary!" The point is that an author does not create new words, but creates a new pattern of words: a poem, an article or a story etc. Even when creating a character in a novel, the author takes different human characteristics and mixes them to create a new character.

This is true for creativity in all fields of human activities. A composer does not create new musical notes nor new musical instruments. But s/he creates a new patterns of notes and rhythms - using a novel combo of vocal music and instruments. That is musical creativity. A brilliant manager does not create human beings. But creates a novel pattern or combination of human talents to create a great organization. So creativity means creating a novel pattern of small already known units.

What is the process of creativity? There are two ways through which a new pattern gets created. One is based on the human mind's ability of imagination. The human mind has an innate ability to create new patterns. The simplest example is speech. Every time you speak a sentence, you are being creative. Every sentence you speak is a novel pattern of words! Everyone is creative when designing her or his home. First, in our minds, we imagine a novel pattern of furniture and other decorations. And then we convert those mental patterns into reality.

But there is another way towards creativity: accidents! There are many examples of accidental creation of novel patterns. Here, the creation of patterns may be accidental.

But the talent lies in recognizing that there is a new and useful creation here. For example, one team in the 3M Company wanted to create a chemical glue. But the experiment turned out to be a flop: the glue would not stick permanently! You could stick two papers with it. But any time later, if you pulled, the papers would come unstuck. What a stupid glue! The disheartened manager kept some tins of it in the secretary's cabin – to be discarded. But the secretary turned out be creative. She started using the glue for temporarily sticking notes to important papers – which could be removed later easily. And, so the tremendously successful 'Post It' sticky notes were born. This was a classic case of an accidental creation of a new pattern – but brilliantly recognized and used by a creative mind.

If you ask, every cook can tell a story of how s/he created a new dish out of accident or perhaps, out of shortage of common ingredients! Of course, every creation is not great or popular. There can be some disastrous creations, too. For example, I wanted to create some new type sweetened rice recipe. So I added prepared coffee to steamed rice. The result was a gastronomic disaster!

The hallmark of a great creative mind is not only creating many new patterns but recognizing which creations would turn out to be great or popular. If you want to develop this ability, it essential to first know the field. It is important to study the wide spectrum of creations in that field created by other people. This helps in two ways. First, it trains the mind to read and talk the ABCs of the field. For example, if you want to be a good poet, you need to read lots of poems written by others. This process creates the templates of poetry in your mind.

Secondly, you come to know what has already been created. Creativity means creating a novel pattern that has not existed before. The opposite of creativity is copying what already exists.

Creativity is the classic symbol of human intelligence. The only other animals that are known to be creative are the birds (and some other animals/ insects) who create their nests.

The creativity is a sign of an active mind. The people, who are 'mentally retired' no longer remain creative. Whereas, some people - who may be quite elderly - remain mentally fresh if they remain creative.

42

The most misunderstood concept of 'Satisfaction'

Looking back at your life, what kind of a feeling would you like: contented, satisfied feeling – or a dissatisfied, discontented, deficient feeling? Think.

But wait a minute: Isn't the modern age dictum like this: 'To become a super-achiever, one has to be constantly hungry'? Aren't these concepts of 'being satisfied' and 'being constantly hungry' opposite? Which one is more true or more important? Are the concepts of 'being satisfied' and 'being hungry' compatible with each other?

The concept of 'satisfaction' is a very commonly misunderstood concept. If a person says, I have led a satisfying life", some people think: "This person has achieved so less in life and yet s/he is feeling satisfied? He (or she) is such a small person"! People equate the concept of satisfaction with being a low-achiever – with a subtle hinting of laziness and smallness! But we can meet people from all strata of life who say, "Yes, I have led a very satisfying life!" So what's their secret?

Satisfaction does not mean 'resting on laurels'. Satisfaction does not mean you will stop trying for more. Satisfaction means you begin each day raring to go and achieve more – but with the contented feeling: "Yes, I have already enjoyed so much, achieved so much so far!" It is a very common observation that happy people can work harder and longer and achieve more. You do not have to have "fire in the belly" of the dissatisfaction type!

It is very important to understand the difference between 'feeling hungry' and 'feeling dissatisfied'.

The persons who carry the dissatisfied type of attitude around make the people around unhappy. They are the most hated people – at home and at work place. On the other hand, people with the satisfied attitude not only make people around happy, but they tend to bring out the best in them. This is because people with the satisfied attitude remember all the good things that the people have done earlier.

A busy, working mother tries to make as healthy and tasty meal – as possible for her. Generally she cooks okay, but occasionally the taste is not up to the mark. What will be the reaction of the people at home? The dissatisfaction attitude people will sharply criticize the lousy food – and leave the mother unhappy and with lower self-esteem.

On the other hand, the people with the satisfied attitude will first remember - and say- all the wonderful dishes the lady had prepared earlier. They will understand that this taste mishap has occurred in spite of the efforts of the lady. This will encourage and make her more determined to prepare a better meal – for the people who remember her earlier good recipes.

A similar tale unfolds at the workplace, too. There are many bosses who are always dissatisfied with the work of the employees. They feel that constantly poking 'the lazy buggers' about the lousy work will make them work harder and longer. It may work in the short term. But in the long run, these are the dissatisfied bosses who make good employees want to leave the company.

In one Psychology experiment, students were given two tests one after the other. After the first test, as a predetermined plan, half the students were soundly criticized and told that they had done poorly in the first test! This was done without consideration of their actual performance. The other half were praised and were told that they had done very well in the first test. Then both the groups were given the second test. The students who experienced the dissatisfaction of the examiners, actually did more poorly in the second test – as compared to the first test. Whereas, the students who were told that the examiners were happy and satisfied about their performance actually did better in the second test – as compared to the first one.

Forget workplace and home and the impact of satisfaction/ dissatisfaction on others. Are you satisfied with yourself? The core concept of satisfaction is remembering all the joys and happiness experienced earlier. Once in a while, do remember all the happy times that you have experienced: All the laughter, all the special moments with dear ones, all your achievements (including the little trophies that you won in school) and all the achievements of your dear ones, all the vacations, all the wonderful movies and music and food, all the times you have helped people and put a smile on their face and so on. Make such a list. Don't forget to write small joys such seeing the flowers bloom in you potted plant!

Once you remember of all these joys, the feeling of happiness and satisfaction is bound to come. Then, in fact, you will feel more energy to go out and add more items to your list!

43

Overcoming the sorrow of bereavement

Mr. and Mrs. Kulkarni lost their only 19 year old son in an accident. As can be imagined, the couple was overcome with grief. And their ages excluded the possibility of conceiving again. Suddenly, a painful, childless future awaited them. But they did not allow their destiny to overpower their spirits. Instead of becoming a depressed, frustrated couple, they put their negative emotions to work. They decided to put their energies and resources to work. They started helping unfortunate children, who were in desperate need of help. Today, they are now looking after the needs of more than 25 children. They are leading a life of satisfaction.

Death of a near one is the ultimate irreversible problem. All of us have to go through the pain. It leads to many types of negative emotions. Some people, like the Kulkarnis, are able to convert the negative emotions into productive efforts. But there are many of us who continue to suffer for a long, long time in various ways. So, it becomes useful to understand the problems and the best ways of overcoming them.

The biggest pain after the death of a loved one is the feeling that I could not save her (or him). Are all deaths avoidable? "If only I knew beforehand, I could have done this or that..." "If the patient herself/ himself or the caregivers had taken more care..." "If only the doctors had done this instead of that ..." Such thoughts can give rise to unending pain. Sometimes, the sadness turns into anger. And that leads to more problems. Anger is always directed at someone (including oneself). We can see many examples, where such anger leads to fights between family members – leading to more misery for all the people involved. The person is gone, but the bitterness between family members persists for many years. It becomes important to realize that no human (including the patient) is perfect. Hence the care cannot be perfect. And that every death cannot be avoided. The only thing to be done is to learn the lesson and use it to help other humans in similar problems. And that is what the relatives of victims of a major fire accident did. They formed a group and had meetings with the fire department, other authorities and the public to improve the prevention and management of fires.

Another major source of pain is the feeling that I wish had spent more time with the departed person. Everyone is busy in their lives. A sudden death leads to a long term sorrow about not doing more for the person when s/he was alive. Some people get transformed by such feelings and become more appreciative of being alive and being with the persons they love. Every day becomes a reminder to relish the company of the loved ones around. It, then, seems wasteful to have petty fights with the loved ones. A perfect example of how negative emotions can lead to positive changes!

The death of a person of a similar age triggers panic in some people. Suddenly death looms large on the horizon. Some people begin to live in fear and lose sleep over whether they will see tomorrow. But then there are other wise people who feel reminded to get their check-ups done. So they go through the battery of tests to find out whether they have any major illness. This leads to early diagnosis and better outcomes. If the reports show that they have no major illness, it frees them from the fears.

Then there are some who develop dark philosophical attitude: What is the use of all that we do when we all are going to die 'one day'? They start living in the shadow of death all the time – and become depressed. Now, consider the life a person who lives for 60 years. This person is going to live for 21,900 days. And will die 'one day'. So, should this person be thinking about 21900 days that s/he is going to live – or think about the 'one day'? We can see many people who live a long, depressed life thinking about that 'one day'! Yes, that one day is truth, but those 21900 days are truths, too! So why not start living all those days to the fullest!

One major type of pain results from guilt. We can see many people who refuse to enjoy, be entertained or even laugh – many years after their loved one has passed away. One mother of two kids remained in mourning even three years after one of the kids passed away. "How can I enjoy when I have lost my son?" Her grief was so intense and persistent that the other child and the husband, too, started becoming depressed.

Death is a reality and grief is normal. We can allow the negative emotions to haunt and depress us. Or we can turn that energy to become better persons.

44
How laughter benefits the mind

The situation is a little tense. One eye has been injured by a cricket ball. Everyone is worried whether vision will come back to normal. A cheery cousin arrives, "Don't bluff, Shrirang. You say it was a ball injury, but I am sure you must have winked at some lady who, then, must have punched you in the eye!" Everyone bursts out laughing. The serious atmosphere has suddenly vaporized. Everyone suddenly feels lighter. Suddenly, it becomes possible to laugh in the face of the problem – even though the problem has not changed. That's the power of laughter.

There are many types and shades of happiness: eating nice food, the joy of listening to melodious music, the peace of watching beautiful scenery, being with loved ones, reading etc. All these types of happiness have the capacity to remove unhappiness. But the most powerful type of happiness is a heartful laughter. It can banish unhappiness the farthest.

We can consider a spectrum of emotions: at one end will be the most intense unhappiness (sadness, fear, anger). In the middle of the spectrum will be calmness or peace. On the other side, the spectrum will extend from mild happiness to max happiness at the end. So if you are experiencing maximum intensity happiness, you will be farthest away from unhappiness. The laughter will be at the tip of the happiness spectrum.

Laughter gives a different perspective to look at the situation. The humorous situation may seem like an extreme perspective, but it helps. Two college friends meet after many years. Raju asks, "You got married?" Sanju says no. Then Raju remembers, "Oh, yeah! You were going to wait for the perfect girl, isn't it? So, you didn't find the perfect girl?" "Yes, I found the perfect girl." Raju: "Then what was the problem? Why didn't you marry her?" Sanju replies sadly, "She was waiting for the perfect man!"

The humour makes us look at the situation from a different angle. It makes us accept the imperfections in ourselves and our lives – with a smile. When we laugh at imperfections or problems, we begin to realize that the situation is not as bad as it initially appeared. We start understanding that we can live peacefully in spite of the problem – and in fact laugh, too.

A friend of mine is – to put it mildly – not good looking. Whenever someone asks him whether he has any brother or sister, he replies in the negative, and says laughingly, "Pitaaji ne sample dekhke aageka order cancel kar diya"! (Father cancelled further order after he saw the sample) The laughter not only allows him to accept the situation, but to live happily in spite of the problem.

When people become upset, they can think of only one point of view – the unhappy point of view. But a different person looking from a wacky perspective shows how it is possible to see the same situation in a different and better and funny light. A friend was going in his car in Mumbai. A man in another car overtook him – while driving quite rashly and rudely. At the next signal, my friend found the other man waiting. He knocked on the other man's car window. The man, expecting a sharp shouting, opened the window. My friend said, "Arre, You are still here? I thought you would have reached Pune by now!" The other man burst out laughing. What could have become an ugly situation, instead became a happy situation because of laughter.

Laughter gives us not only the strength to face problems but to turn the tables around. A very simple, common situation: you are walking on the road and you slip and fall down. What would be your reaction? Would you become angry thinking that people are looking at you and you have made a fool of yourself? Or will you laugh heartily, get up, brush your clothes and get on?

Undoubtedly, creating laughter by making fun of people can be a risky sometimes. If the other person gets offended, it can lead to revenge. But if people, especially friends, enjoy making fun of each other, it can lead to great bonding! Pulling each other's legs and doing practical jokes can be great if everyone becomes a butt of the jokes some time or the other. If only one person is targeted, it can lead to a lot of ill-feeling.

Every emotion has a group of thoughts and thinking patterns linked to it. For example, a sad mood leads to hopelessness, guilt, negative expectations about the future and so on. But laughter brings on all the positive thoughts: enthusiasm, hopefulness, bonding, tolerance etc.

The Laughter Clubs are a good idea because it makes people decide to laugh every day. And they do so without waiting for some funny event to happen.

I am sure the world will be a much, much better place if everyone started laughing more!

45
Wishful thinking

All of us have, literally, hundreds of wishes. "I wish my child does well in his career", "I wish I'll look good when I go for that function", "I wish I get a lenient examiner". There are so many more: 'I wish my Mom and Dad don't fight with each other", "I wish I don't get bedridden", "I wish this lead character of this movie (or a serial) is able to fulfil her wish in the next episode". The list of wishes is practically unending: 'the wish to get that promotion', 'the wish to do some good for the unfortunate people', 'the wish to teach that person a lesson', 'the wish to eat chocolate ice cream with lots of nuts', 'the wish to kill the persons of the other community' and so on and on and on.

How do we acquire all these hundreds of wishes? Are we born with all these wishes? Are they implanted in our minds by other people? Can we control what wishes we should have?

We have many 'instinctual' wishes: wishes that are inborn. All the animals have these instinctual wishes, too. There are several types of these instinctual wishes. For example, consider the wish to eat and drink. The wish to enjoy sexual pleasure is an important instinctual wish necessary for the propagation of a species. The wish to enjoy 'sensory' pleasures (pleasures related to the different senses- eyes, ears, nose, tongue, skin etc.) is a huge category of wishes. The wish to avoid pain and discomfort is another instinctual wish.

We humans have the 'wish to create'. We have created uncountable number of objects. But this 'wish to create' is not the exclusive property of humans alone. Many animals, birds and even insects have this 'wish to create'. They, too, create their homes (nests) that are amazingly complex. Another basic wish is the 'wish to possess (or own)'. Even the animals have the wish own a territory – a patch of land and the resources. They, too, valiantly defend their homelands from intruders!

We humans have a very important instinctual wish to get respect and love from others – family members and everyone around - at work, in the neighbourhood (local or online). For some, getting respect from others is so important that they may resort to violence to ensure respect for the leader. This is true, not only for the gorillas, but for some human leaders, too!

'The wish to take revenge', 'the wish of curiosity (wish to know)', 'the wish to play games' and even the 'wish to make others happy' are instinctual wishes that can be seen even in animals. As can be seen, these instinctual wish categories are only a few. But how do all the hundreds of wishes that each of us has, arise?

Although the instinctual wishes are only a few, they get transformed into all the hundreds of wishes. Consider the simple instinctual 'wish to eat'. Suppose you are hungry when visiting a friend. The friend serves you a new type of sweet dish. You relish it. Then and there, you have acquired a new wish: the wish to eat that particular type sweet dish. Similarly, you may have developed the wish to eat so many other types of recipes, too. So, the single instinctual 'wish to eat' has got transformed into so many different wishes to eat so many types of foods. This was the result of you yourself enjoying the food first and then developing the wish.

Sometimes we develop a wish just by observing others enjoying something. Many of the ads use this method. You see an actor gulping a drink – glug, glug, glug – and then saying, "AAAAHH" with a broad smile of satisfaction on his face! Your instinctual desire to drink has just got transformed into 'wish to drink and enjoy what that actor has enjoyed'! It's not just kids who can be mesmerized like this. Adults, too, can be made to develop different wishes by showing the enjoyment of others. In fact, all of us 'promote' different joys, pleasures, happinesses to people around, "Go to that Godman (or Godwoman), and you will find mental peace." And so on.

Sometimes we acquire many wishes as 'steps-wishes'. Let me explain. Suppose, a girl sees the Badminton world champion in action – playing against world opponents and winning and enjoying praises from all. So this girl develops the desire to be a champion like her. This results in her developing many new wishes: wish to get up early, wish to practise hard, follow a diet and so on. So the basic 'wish to be a champion' resulted in all these wishes.

And thus, we acquire all the hundreds of wishes. I am sensing that you, the reader, has acquired a new wish: 'the wish that I end this Wishipedia'. So, I think I should stop now!

46
Adaptability: the great human ability

"My daughter is going away for studies to a distant land far away from us. I hope she will be able to adapt to the new place and new people – and do well in studies. I don't know about her, but I am going to terribly miss her – becoming a kind of homesick myself!" These could be the words of a parent whose child has gone from a small remote village to a faraway city or they could be the words of a parent whose child has gone abroad. Will the daughter adapt to the new life? Will the parent adapt to the life without the daughter? What exactly is 'adaptability'?

Adaptability doesn't just mean learning a new language or acclimatizing to different weather conditions. It means a whole lot of changes that happen in the mind – in the process of successfully mastering a new situation. It is very important to realize that adapting does not mean meekly and sadly accepting a new situation. It means developing new skills and achieving what one wants – even in the new circumstances.

We humans are master adapters. Even if we just consider different geographical or climactic conditions, humans have been able to live successfully in all corners of the world – and even in space! No other animal can adapt so well to such diverse environments.

Bu we humans face varieties of challenging living conditions that are not just atmospheric. Getting married or having children are adaptability challenges – and so also losing one's spouse by divorce or death. Managing a new job is always a challenge. But losing one's job - especially in the middle age - is a bigger challenge. This is becoming commoner in today's turbulent business environment. Sudden major health problems in oneself or the dear ones, test our adaptability to the extreme. Such challenges are faced by everyone – from the poorest to the richest.

What are the specific mental abilities that allow us to successfully adapt to all the varieties of changes? And why is it that some people are unable to adapt and become miserable? A lot depends on how we view the situation. There are opposing perspectives on any change: the comfort of a 'normal' routine versus the uncertainty of the change; the boredom of the same old life versus the excitement of the novel experiences! Do you look at the new situation as a problem or a challenge? The final outcome of the 'adaptability contest' depends on the mindset of the person: the beliefs, the wishes and the emotions.

If a person believes that the change is a terrible calamity, then it will be difficult for the person to adapt successfully. If the person believes in her/ his adaptability, then s/he will put in all the efforts to adapt. It is very important to look at the change as an opportunity to grow and improve. For example, consider a man who has been transferred by his company to another town. Undoubtedly, there will be discomforts, but the family can look at it as an opportunity to develop new skills. Children who relocate to a new town can become smarter and more able at developing friendships. Persons who are exposed to a variety of people and situations can become more mature and can understand the broad spectrum of life. Why humans, even rats in the laboratory have been shown to develop bigger brains if they are exposed to complex environment as compared to simple, mundane environment!

Not only the beliefs, but wishes, too, determine whether you will be able adapt successfully. The most important wish is the wish to learn new skills and knowledge. For example, consider a sudden, major disability (such as paralysis) that alters the lifestyle. Earlier, the life is smoother. But the arrival of an illness leads to major changes and restrictions in the lifestyle. Here, the determination or an intense wish to make the life as normal as possible makes the person learn new skills – skills to overcome the limitations by adapting new strategies. Then there are people who simply accept the defeat and the restrictions.

The emotion status plays a major role in the adaptation process. The person with a strong happiness can not only adapt better but can actually enjoy the process of transformation. The person who has a happy mindset picks up the advantages better than an unhappy person who will selectively count all the problems associated with the transition. Consider a simple common situation. A student has to go to different town for studies. The student with the unhappy mindset will feel sad about going away from old friends. The person with the happy mindset will look forward to making new friends – while keeping in touch with old friends on mobile.

The life has many twists and turns. If we turn on our adaptability, we can come out winners!

47

"I am not addicted to alcohol!"

Typical scene in the doctor's consulting room. Wife requests doctor: "Please do something for my husband's alcohol addiction." Husband denies: "Oh, no! I am not an addict. I am in full control of my alcohol intake. I never exceed my three large pegs in the evening. I can give it up any time I decide to. I gave it up last year, isn't it?" Wife: "The problem is that he never decides to give up! Last year, he stopped for a month when his friend died of alcohol-related complications."

This person had not touched alcohol till seventeen years of age. So how did he reach this stage? What happens in the mind of people with addictions to alcohol, cigarette / tobacco or other drugs of abuse such as marijuana? It doesn't happen in a day. So how does a person come into the grip of addiction?

It happens gradually, in stages. It commonly begins in teenage. With the wish of curiosity: how does the high of the cigarette or alcohol feel? And the journey into addiction begins. The younger the teenager, more is the chance of him or her becoming an addict.

The teenager sees rich and successful and apparently healthy people consuming alcohol. So s/he naively assumes that alcohol is safe. The naiveté prevents him or her from realizing that they are rich and successful and apparently healthy - not because of alcohol but in spite of it.

All the addicting substances are basically some chemical compounds that get absorbed into the blood and reach the brain. There they act on the nerve cells. One of effects of these chemicals is the peculiar feeling of high that lasts for some time. That's it!

All the other descriptions and discussions about the type of alcohol (whiskey versus beer etc.) or the types of cigarettes / cigars etc. are only related to taste while it is in the mouth. Once the chemical reaches the blood and the brain, only two things matter: the amount of the chemical (such as alcohol or nicotine) and the duration it stays in the brain. Larger the amount of the chemical, bigger is the effect.

Once the teenager experiences the high, the wish to experience the high again and again develops.

Most of the people are aware of the 'side effects' of these chemicals and the addiction on mind, body, family and career. Thus there is a tug of war in the mind between wish to consume (alcohol etc.) and the wish to avoid these side effects.

Gradually, the person starts consuming the substance more often: from once in few months to every weekend. The person who realizes the importance of avoiding alcohol on week days, generally remains a social drinker. This person looks at alcohol (or other substances) as one of the many types of enjoyment that life offer and can live happily without consuming alcohol (etc.) – while enjoying all the other wonderful joys.

The next stage is the main problem stage. Here gradually alcohol starts replacing other joys as the main source of pleasure. Then wish to drink becomes stronger and stronger. The person starts consuming it more than once a week. More and more excuses are found for drinking: a friend has come > drink to give him company; India won the match > drink to celebrate; India lost the match: drink to drown the blues etc.

In this stage, the glorification of alcohol increases: 'alcohol is a wonderful friend', 'the person who drinks is a great connoisseur' etc. And without realizing, the person's frequency becomes three times or more per week. Danger starts!

As the addiction worsens, the pleasure of the kick the person gets with one peg becomes less. So, to get the same high, s/he starts drinking more: two, three – up to six pegs. Interestingly, this is taken as a sign of 'manliness' or 'strength': "I can drink so much and yet remain standing!!" Actually, it is not a sign of strength but the level of addiction: s/he needs more alcohol to get the same kick or to get drunk.

At this stage, the hangover and withdrawal symptoms become more severe. The mood is more irritable and depressed when the alcohol is not in the brain. So the person starts drinking just to feel normal. The mood swings. The health starts deteriorating.

The person may stop for a few days if the health is affected. But starts drinking again as soon as health improves a little.

It you drink alcohol (or consume other substances), find out where you are in this sequence of stages. Remember the frequency in your earlier days. That will tell you where your trajectory is headed.

One last point: discourage - and definitely don't encourage - teenagers to drink or smoke.

48
Some interesting insights about 'feeling bored'!

An old dictum: How to make an interesting novel boring? Put it as a compulsory reading in school or college!

A parent enthusiastically tells the child, "Sachin uncle and Pooja aunty are going to visit us today evening along with their kids!" The child frowns, "Oh, no! They are so boring. I will be wasting two hours of my life."

When you go work each morning, do you feel happy that you will be doing something interesting – or do you feel that the work is so boring but you have to do it in order to earn the salary?

Feeling bored is an integral part of our mental life. A lot of our activities and efforts are spent for avoiding boredom. Is it just a normal passing phase – or can it be a sign of a problem such as depression? Or is it a good motivation for us to become creative and do something good? What are the reasons for boredom and how can we overcome it?

It is definitely true that one major reason for boredom is our attitude. There are three kinds of attitudes towards boredom. The first is the Anti-Boring Attitude (also known as Enthu / Humorous Attitude). The people who have this attitude never get bored. For them, every activity is interesting. Or they find a funny angle to look at what is obviously a boring activity. Or they amuse themselves with some side fun.

The famous humorous writer of yesteryears, P. G. Wodehouse, was imprisoned by the Germans in World War II, when he was nearly sixty years of age. At that age, when he was already a famous and popular writer, he was given the horrible duty of cleaning the prison toilets. But his humorous spirit would not get dampened by the ugly situation. He kept on cracking jokes and describing the situation in a funny way. These funny descriptions were broadcast by the Berlin Radio. It almost lead some crazy British people into thinking that P. G. Wodehouse was actually having fun in the German jail! So much so, that these people started saying that he had defected to the German side and should be called a traitor! There cannot be a better example of a strong attitude triumphing over the –not just boring – but horrible situation.

The opposite attitude is the BASA –"Boring Angle Seeking Attitude"! The people who have this attitude will find something boring in the midst of many interesting things. These people, when faced with a lavish wedding dinner spread, will manage to find some salad which is salty – and hence boring! Of course, the star players in this BASA team are the kids who find all home-made food boring, all books boring, all cousins boring and even the gifts they receive boring!

Then there is a third attitude IASHS –TYAB Attitude ("I Am So High Standard – That You Are Boring" Attiude!) The persons with this attitude find it below their dignity to laugh at jokes which make most people laugh a lot. "What stupid jokes you like". The flip side of this coin is that "Your joke was so boring". As a result, these people remain bored most of the time. They are never happy with the dresses they buy because "the brands I prefer were not available in that (lowly) mall".

Boredom isn't always bad. One possible good side-effect of boredom is that it can spark creativity. You must have experienced this. A bunch of kids get together to play as usual. But then someone says, "It is so boring to play the same thing again and again." Others reluctantly agree. Now what to do? Then the creative side of their minds starts working. Soon they create a new game (or a new modification of an old game) and have a lot of fun!

School or college studies can be considered to be the winner of the "Most Commonly Boring Activity" competition! There are many reasons that make it boring. As described above, compulsion has the property of making anything boring. Long hours of studying also are responsible. Seemingly repetitive activities make it boring. There is one another hidden reason that can make studies boring: if a kid has not understood a topic or subject, s/he will find it boring. Parents and teachers should look for this reason when a child finds a particular subject boring.

It is important to realize that "feeling bored all the time" can be a symptom of depression! Some people with depression don't feel sad overtly. But they 'lose interest' in doing activities that they used to enjoy earlier. They may say that nowadays they find all those activities 'boring'. The key to differentiate between 'normal' boredom and this boredom, is that the same activities that seemed interesting earlier, now seem boring – and nothing seems interesting.

Reading long articles can be very boring. So before you get bored, let me stop writing ...!

49
The curious case of Curiosity

"Wow! The movie was fantastic! Absolutely edge of the seat - till the end." If the director can keep the curiosity alive –"What's going to happen now??"- throughout the movie, it becomes a hit. Nowadays teens threaten their friends, "I will send you the spoiler!" – meaning, "I will reveal what happens at the end of the movie". Nobody wants it because this means killing the curiosity.

Curiosity is a basic instinctual wish found even in animals. All the birds and animals are continually curious – and hence they are able to survive! Because they are curious about the surrounding world, they can find food. And it is the curiosity that teaches them about the dangers. For example, lion cubs are quite curious (and careful) about snakes. They need to know whether the snake means food or danger. But, traditionally, the brand ambassador of curiosity has been cat! Cats are extremely curious about all things. It is this curiosity about the area that gets them mice – and shelter for the babies. When the cat is pregnant, its curiosity helps her to find out the safest mini cave for delivery and rearing the kittens.

But we humans are actually more curious creatures than cats. The curiosity took explorers to all corners of the world – and even into the depths of ocean and into the space. The curiosity made us scientists. The fantastic progress that we have made is the result of the systematic, focused curiosity of the scientists – for both discoveries and inventions. "What will happen if we do this?" The tremendous desire for experimentation is not limited to just scientists and engineers. Every cook has this curiosity to know how a new permutation and combination recipe will taste. This has resulted in such a wide variety of recipes that we enjoy now.

The curiosity wish has made us not only scientists and explorers, but also gossipers! The wish to know what is happening in the lives of others is a major wish for humans. But our curiosity about other people is not limited to gossiping about dirty politics or for showing somebody down. It helps us in many ways. We keep learning from others' experiences. We become smarter by knowing how other people have tackled various problems. One other benefit of is this: knowing about others' problems and misfortunes motivates many of us to go ahead and help them.

The media and the social media have expanded our circles of gossip. We can come to know what is happening to whom in all parts of the world. Every day it is the curiosity that drives us to open the newspaper and the social media. The curiosity leads to a positive cycle: our curiosity leads us to know more about certain people or topics. And then, because we know more about them, we are more curious about them. For example, if you know more about politicians or actors or players or businesspeople etc., you will be more curious to know what is happening to them. So you will read more about them. Think: who are the people that you read about with a lot of interest?

One peculiar type of curiosity is the curiosity about dangerous and horrible things. It is this wish that drives people to go and watch horror movies. 'What can horrible creatures or ghosts do? What terrible fates can people undergo?' Such curious questions drive the interest in horror movies. The curiosity about dangers is a useful instinctual wish. But it takes a srange turn in this topic.

The children are full of questions because they are curious. What? Why? When? Where? Which? How? Sometimes the adults get fed up of the endless questions. But we must remember that it is the curiosity that makes the children learn fast. When they lose the curiosity, learning becomes boring. If the parents and teachers can ignite and channelize the innate curiosity of the children, they can become the best coaches.

The curiosity is equally important at the other end of the life spectrum. We can observe that some of the elder are 'mentally retired' and are leading routine, boring lives. On the other hand, we can see many lively elders who are leading enriching lives. What is the difference between these two groups? The people who are mentally active and lively, are the elders who still have a lot of curiosity! They want to learn new skills, new technologies such mobiles and computers. They are still curious about the wonders of the world. With a positive attitude, they are interested in all the people. The curiosity is the heart of the motivation engine that keeps them going. The curiosity and the interest in learning new things, actually keeps the aging process in the brain at bay. So be curious and be healthy!

50
What freedom means ..

"I live in a free country where I can do anything I want – except what my wife, my parents, my children, my neighbours, my boss, my doctor, my dentist, my banker, my lawyer, the police, the traffic police, my religious leaders and my PR people tell me not to do!" That's freedom!

What is 'freedom' – and the loss of freedom? Every human activity and concept arises from the mind and has impact on the minds. So, if we want to know what freedom (and loss of freedom) means, we need to understand it in terms of the mind and its events.

So, freedom means the freedom to fulfil all the wishes. The loss of freedom is when we are not allowed to fulfil our wishes.

There are many parts of the mind: beliefs, wishes, emotions, the attention of the mind and the mental abilities. But out of all these, the wishes are the closest to the 'I'. We can almost say that the 'I' is made up of all the wishes that each of us has. We can give up our beliefs, we can give up our emotions. But if we have to give up our wishes, it almost feels like somebody is tearing out a part of our body. For example, consider a student whose exams are very near.

The preparation has not been good. The parents tell her to give up using her mobile for a few weeks. But the wish to use the mobile is so strong that the child feels that it is like the pain of amputation!

There was this alcohol addicted guy who came back from the doctor's clinic with a serious look on his face. He tells his wife, "Every time I visit the doctor, he tells me stop alcohol. So, finally, I have decided to stop…" The wife smiles with a pleasant surprise … The guy continues, "… So, finally, I have decided to stop … going to that doctor!" Any person, who asks somebody to give up a wish, is sure to become unpopular!

A friend of mine was telling me why he doesn't like dieticians in general. This is because they tell clients to give up eating this, give up eating that etc. He says, he liked one dietician because she never made him give up any of his wishes. Instead she was positive: she asked him to start taking various things – like lemon and honey in water in the mornings! Now, don't ask me how much weight he lost, but he continued with the dietician for a long time!

This freedom desire is almost instinctual. Even six-month old babies show this. For example, a baby is happily lying on the bed, constantly moving the arms and legs. You just try and hold the baby's arms close to the body – in order to prevent the baby from moving. Soon, the baby will start howling in protest – because of losing the freedom to move the arms as s/he pleases! You let go of the arms and the baby regains the freedom to move the arms and immediately the smile returns!

We used to have a pet dog that was always free to roam inside the house. But when some guests, who did not like dogs, would come, we had to tie him with a leash. He could lie down comfortably in his favourite spot with the leash. But, no! He would start barking in protest so much that we had to untie him. As soon as he was untied, he would go and happily lie down at exactly the same favourite spot – but, now without the leash! That dog did not want his freedom – the wish to roam wherever he wanted – to be curtailed!

Any punishment basically means restricting some of the wishes of the person being punished. For example, suppose a parent want to punish a child who has misbehaved. So, she says, "No TV for you for two days." This means antagonizing a dear wish of the chid. The ultimate punishment is when a judge sends a criminal to prison. It means loss of freedom - to fulfil so many wishes: the wish to go where one wants, the wish to meet whoever one wants, the wish to enjoy various entertainments, attend functions etc. Considering this concept, all the cages of all the animals and birds can be considered to be prisons! The only rational use of cages is when the animal or bird has to be kept for treatment.

Jokingly, many people call a marriage as a loss of freedom – as compared to the bachelor days (and bachelorette days)! Both the parties have to let go of so many wishes – in exchange for fulfilling so many other wishes.

So, there is nothing like 'complete freedom'! Freedom basically means fulfilling the desires we want – while giving up the wishes we don't mind giving up!

51

'Generalizing' – the necessary evil!

Three persons are traveling in a car in a different state. They see a black cow. First person says, "All cows in this state are black. " The second one says, "All we can say is that there is at least one black cow in this state." The third person says, "The only conclusion we can draw is that there is at least one cow in this state whose one side is black!" It is so easy to laugh at the first person. But so many times, we tend to draw conclusions like him.

Consider elections – our favourite pastime! "This leader is great." "That leader is a crook." "That one is a fool"! Our generalizations come freely and fast! And after we have concluded, we pick up the media titbits that agree with our conclusions – while ignoring the titbits that are opposite to our conclusions! And so our conclusions – that are gross generalizations – continue happily!

Most of us intelligent people recognize the fallacy of quick and gross generalizations. Yet we continue to do it all the time. We generalize about people, situations, predictions and even about our lives! Our generalizations help us to process information fast but many a times they result in disastrous consequences. So it is important to understand this thing called generalizing that is so much a part of daily life.

The main result of generalizing is that it produces labels. "That person is unreliable. Don't ask her/him to do important work." "That person is an egotist." "S/he is stupid." And so on. How do we come to such conclusions? We come in contact with some people for a short time – few hours or even a few minutes. And yet that is enough for us to draw conclusions about that person. Sometimes we do not even meet a person (e.g. political leaders or other famous people). And yet we put labels. Is this type of generalization correct or wrong? We have to deal with people all the time. So it becomes very important to draw some conclusions about persons – in order to decide how we are going to behave with them. So even if we do not have enough information about the person, we need to derive conclusions quickly. So, fast generalizations about people become essential.

Generalization or labelling becomes very important when we have to select and appoint a person – as an employee or an MLA or – even as the son or daughter-in-law! Labels are easier to handle – than large amounts of complex information. Suppose you want to employ a maid. You come to know that earlier she was previously employed by a friend. So, naturally you ask that person how she is. Now, what kind of an answer would you like: a quick generalization or a balanced, detailed analysis of her personality? Suppose the friend says, "She is okay as far as the work is concerned. She works quite hard – provided she comes to work regularly. She has a habit of taking leave suddenly. She is quite honest but is quite talkative. She will keep talking with us and even other maids. One day, what happened was ..." Etc. etc. etc. Your friend can go on talking and give you so much information that you get confused. Finally, in exasperation, you ask, "Is she suitable to be employed with us?" And the friend might say, "No, she is not a good maid." Now, that is a sweeping generalization or labelling – but it is useful for you! While you are aware that it is not a precise description of the maid's complex personality, it is easier to handle.

One peculiar feature of our 'liberal' times is to call someone 'judgmental'. Suppose you are talking about some celebrity. And you say, "She is crazy! She did such and such thing!" If there is a liberal person in the group, s/he will immediately call you judgmental or having labelling attitude. The funny part of it is that the moment that liberal person calls you judgmental (or labelling), s/he herself/himself is being judgmental about you – by putting a label on you!

We keep making generalizations about different situations or future or about our life, too. Suppose you ask your son about the speech he gave in his school. He says, "It was a fiasco. I mispronounced the name of our chief guest." Now, this 'fiasco' is a gross generalization that is quite wrong because according to his teachers, he spoke very well – apart from the small error.

When we become emotional, we tend to do quick generalizations that are likely to be wrong. When emotional, people tend to make sweeping generalizations about future and life. For example, a break up can make a teenager conclude that life is not worth living, and that the entire future is going to be unhappy. Such sweeping generalizations make some people attempt suicide.

On the other hand, a major achievement can make a person believe that s/he can indeed have a great future – leading that person to work hard and really achieve it!

So, generalizations are here to stay. But we need to be aware of the shortcomings.

52

Are you 'sensitive' – or 'delicate'?

"I am a very sensitive person. I cannot tolerate people's insensitive, rude behaviour. It makes me cry immediately. There are people who are thick-skinned. But I am not one."

What is the meaning of 'being a sensitive person'? Is it the same as the sensitive nature of poets? Is it a special and desirable quality? Is 'being thick-skinned' the opposite of 'being sensitive'?

Some of the poets, writers, directors or artistes are known as 'sensitive'. They are able to identify and portray very fine and subtle differences between human feelings and experiences. For example, a sensitive actor can understand and display the difference between childlike and childish behaviour of a character. Or a sensitive dialogue writer can understand and write the speech of a character that shows apparently loving words but dry feelings. This is the 'poetic sensitivity' that is quite desirable – not only in an author or actor, but in every person.

But consider the 'emotional sensitivity' that was described in the first paragraph. For example, there is a classroom, A teacher is telling about the answers written by a student. The teacher uses a slightly harsh word and the student starts crying. Now, is this 'being sensitive'? Is this the 'poetic sensitivity'? Here the student is being delicate. A slightly harsh breeze and the flower falls down.

It is useful and interesting to understand what happens in the mind when it encounters a slightly unpleasant situation. Suppose you are walking down the footpath in a normal, calm mood. By chance, you bang against someone and his belongings fall down. So he utters a few bad words. You say sorry and help him and then you move on. Now, what happens to your mood? Do you 'take the problem in your stride'- meaning you continue to be in your calm mood? Or, do you get into a foul mood? This is the test that will tell you whether you are strong or 'delicate'.

Suppose you get into a little unpleasant emotion. But you are able to control it soon and get back into your original calm mood, then you are strong. But, if your unpleasant emotion lingers on and becomes the unpleasant mood, then you are 'delicate'. We need to understand the proportion between the severity of the problem and he intensity of the emotional reaction. Major problems can push anyone into a unhappy mood. But a small problem pushes you into an unhappy mood, then it is not 'being sensitive', but 'being delicate'.

Then, is it better to be 'thick-skinned' and 'insensitive'? Suppose, you have a two-years old child. Every time the child falls, should you immediately rush to pick up and comfort the child to make her stop crying as soon as possible? If you don't rush every time, are you being insensitive? If you have a desire to make the child strong, independent and self-sufficient, then you may observe the child. You may deliberately decide to ignore the child's crying and prod her to get up on her own. This is being 'sensitive' (to the child's plight) but, you may appear 'insensitive' to a third observer.

Being a little thick-skinned is definitely advantageous. Nobody's life is fully smooth and pothole-free. Everyone goes through unpleasant interactions with the people around. If you are 'delicate', then you will go through frequent bouts of unpleasant mood. Every small unpleasantness in an interaction will disturb you.

But if you are a little thick-skinned, then you can calmly walk your way through such unpleasant interactions and achieve your goal. You must have observed many ugly quarrels – between colleagues, between sellers and customers and at home, too. If a person is cool ('thick-skinned'), s/he can take the verbal punches better. This person finally controls the situation. So being a little thick-skinned helps.

However, if a person is 'insensitive' type of thick-skinned, then s/he will bulldoze the way through – leaving a lot of wounded people in the process. This is obviously an undesirable quality. But sometimes we have to take decisions that are going to make some people (colleagues, family members or others) unhappy either way. If the choice is Option 1, then person A is going to be unhappy. If the choice is Option 2, then person B is going to become upset. The 'delicate' person goes through endless agony trying to take such a decision. Being a little thick-skinned becomes necessary in such situations.

What can a 'delicate' person do to become stronger? Learning to keep the emotion circuits under control is one important method. But accepting that different people have different natures is equally important. All five fingers are not alike. Each person behaves according to her or his personality and moods. No one, – even a dictator – cannot change all people. Accepting this fact is useful for one's pace of mind.

So, being 'delicate' and 'insensitive' are two opposite undesirable extremes. But being 'sensitive' – and a little thick-skinned seems to be the best option!

53
The small pleasures of life

I was walking on the road. I noticed a small kitten – a cute sight. But what was cuter was a small three years old girl squatting next to the kitten and reciting – almost teaching – the nursery rhyme, "Pussy cat, Pussy cat, where have you been…"! The kid is totally sincere and engrossed and in full flow with all the gestures, while communicating with the kitten. And the kitten? It's looking at the kid with an amused expression! That unforgettable sight made my day. And, in fact, even now, it makes my day whenever I remember it!

I am sure you will be able tell so many such wonderful or funny or heart-warming or mind-cooling small stories. "I reached that hill station at night. And when I woke up the next morning and went out into the verandah, my god, what a beautiful scene!" You will certainly remember different recipes that you have enjoyed at different places. These cannot be called be called the Big Pleasures of life – like marriage, getting the first job or promotion or getting admission into the coveted college or buying a new home etc. But these small joys have an immensely important place in our lives.

The Big Desires and Big Pleasures are certainly important. We spend a great deal of our time and efforts in fulfilling those wishes. It is also true, that after all the hard work, the happiness of having achieved is great. It keeps us happy and proud for a long time. But these Big Joys don't happen every day. (For example, how many times do you get the joy of getting married?!)

But the small joys are different. They keep coming our way so often. Somebody cracking a joke is one such Small Joy. If you have cracked the joke and made people laugh, then the joy is much bigger! There are many such small pleasures. Listening to or humming wonderful songs can give so much pleasure. Watching a beautiful piece of acting by an actor or watching a master player in action gladdens the heart.

There are many times when we are looking forward to that joyous event such as a favourite TV show. But many, many times life gives us pleasant surprises – like the story of the girl and the kitten. We are passing by a house and we suddenly see a beautiful flowering plant and, perhaps some butterflies. There are two types of reactions to such a sight. One reaction is a flat unemotional response, "So what's great about the flowers? Haven't you seen flowers before? I am not a kid now. I am too mature to enjoy such silly things." Then there are some others who will relish all such beauties that nature offers. No prizes for guessing which of these two people will lead a happier life?

It is important to realize that one has to have a receptive mind to pick up and enjoy such small pleasures. My daughter is one such raconteur or storyteller. She will tell the story of how the teacher scolded a classmate with such funny details that you may think that she has been to a stand-up comedian's show! A jolly mind can pick up such small joys easily. But a depressed or anxious or irritated mind is not receptive to all such small joys that come our way. Can you understand the trick that the mind plays in his matter? If you are in a happy mood, you pick up and enjoy all the small joys – becoming happier in the process. Whereas, if you are in an unhappy mood (sad, fearful, angry), then you don't pick up or enjoy the small pleasures. Either way, the mood is self-perpetuating. The happy mood will continue and so will the unhappy mood.

So what's the moral of the story? Start enjoying all the small pleasures. They will keep adding to your bucket of happiness and help to get into that cheerful mood that everyone wants. On the other hand, if you are unable to enjoy the small pleasures, check yourself. Is an unhappy mood the reason? Then put in all your efforts to change that.

It is true that many of us get many problems in life. Sometimes, counting the problems leads to the feeling that 'my life is full of problems – and there is no happiness in my life'. This thinking is a hallmark of depression. When problems come - and the Big Joys don't come, this conclusion seems real. But here the person is forgetting all the small pleasures. Just as the problems come, the small pleasures, too, come into our life all the time. This is the realistic, balanced view of life.

The best part of the small pleasures is that they are not 'achievements'! We don't have to put in a lot of efforts to get them. We just have to notice them – and ENJOY!

54

Why should we learn about the mind?

What is it that determines whether a person will become a rock star or a shopkeeper or a saint or a terrorist? Is it the height or the size of the biceps or the skin texture? Obviously, it is the mind that decides what a person will become. The mind is clearly the most important aspect of any person's personality.

Forget about achievements, what is it that determines whether a person will become happy or unhappy? It is not the colour of the eyes or the type of hair, but it is the mindset that leads to happiness or unhappiness. And, of course, the happiness, sadness, fear and anger are parts of the mind itself!

I was talking to Mr. Rajendra Singh, a senior HR manager of a large company. This person has interviewed thousands of people and recruited hundreds of them. He has followed up the careers of hundreds of people. His special topic of interest is predicting who will rise in a company and who get stuck - and who will probably be fired! So I asked him what it is that determines this. Is it the type of education?

His answer was a clear, "No"! He said that it is the mindset of the person that leads to achievement or non-achievement. So, when he recruits people, he doesn't pay much attention to the qualifications, but to what is there in the minds of the people.

On the other hand, what is it that determines whether a person will become a terrorist who opens gunfire on a crowd or a person who dedicates his life to help the poorest? What is it that determines whether a person will develop mental disorder or not? The answer, again, is the mindset.

Suppose, you are a young man wanting to get married and you are looking for a bride. Will you choose a beautiful girl with a nasty mind or a plain looking girl with a loving mind? Beauty will give you happiness for some time. But when you are thinking in terms of years and decades of married life, the charm of beauty will wear out soon. But the beauty of the mind will continue to give happiness throughout the life.

Just think of what you yourself do all day? Right from the time you get up to the time you fall asleep, what you are using continuously is the mind. Even if you are just relaxing with your eyes closed, you mind is still active – daydreaming of this and that and that and that! At that time, you are not moving any muscles (except, of course, the breathing muscles). You are not aware of your heart pumping or intestines digesting or bone marrow making blood. But you are very much aware of all the thoughts, wishes and emotions in your mind.

Your mind is the theatre where all this drama is happening all the time 24*7! You learn about all the events in your world, you feel all the emotions, you make choices and control all the actions that you do. Whether you enjoy or become upset, it all happens in your mind. Thus mind is the most important part of our body and personality.

All the intelligent, educated people like you and me know many things about the body: cholesterol and sugar, vitamins and calcium, bones and heart and liver and kidneys etc. etc. We all know that intestines digest food. We learnt about all this, way back in the early years of the school. But we did not learn about what the mind is made up of or how it works - in school. We did not learn how the different emotions are produced in response to different events in our lives in school curriculum. Unfortunately, we are not taught about all these most important aspects of our life in school. And yet these are the most important topics that govern our lives. And explaining that is the purpose of this series on Mind Matters.

One basic perspective about the mind is that it processes information. For example, our entire day and life is made up of small, small topics. The mind deals with each topic one after the other throughout the day. For example, consider the simple topic of 'you noticing a speck of dirt on your shirt sleeve'. Your eyes send information about the dirt on the sleeve to the mind. The mind immediately compares it with your 'wish to remain clean'. Oops! This is against your wish. This leads to the production of emotion: you feel irritated. The next step is decision-making: you decide to remove that speck of dirt. And bang! Your mind has given order for action to your hand. Swish, swish, and the dirt is gone. Your 'wish to remain clean' is fulfilled. And you become happy again! This is how our mind processes each of the inputs that it receives.

Hence, it is important – and very useful – to learn about mind, how it works and how problems can develop in the mind and what can we do to prevent and solve those problems.

55

The subtle difference between positive and negative wishes

We humans have so many instinctive wishes: right from 'wish to eat and drink', 'wish to enjoy sex' 'wish to enjoy sensual pleasures', 'wish to create', 'wish to take revenge', 'wish to get respect and love' and so on. All these wishes can be seen in animals, too, – though not all in one animal. For example, most birds have the 'wish to create (their nests)'! If we humans have inherited these wishes from our ancestors, then they are good for our survival. But are they all good and positive – or are some of them negative?

Some of these wishes immediately seem negative. For example, consider the 'wish to take revenge'. Whenever we become angry, we try to find out who is responsible for the problem and who is to be blamed for the problem. And then, the 'wish to take revenge' becomes active: "You have hurt me, so I want to hurt you". This wish takes on many names: punishment, teaching a lesson and so on. All the laws are completely based on the concept of punishment. Is 'punishing' a positive wish or negative? There are three parts of punishment: first is the 'wish for revenge': "I have suffered, so now you must suffer". The second component is that the punishment should serve as a deterrent – to others who may be thinking of committing the same offence. The third part is compensation to the victim. Now, you can decide which part of this 'wish to punish' is positive or negative.

Consider another very common wish: the 'wish to win a match or competition'. We say, 'healthy competition', isn't it? The 'wish to win' is a positive wish because it motivates us to become more skilled. So, if all the competitors have this wish, all of them grow in caliber. But, suppose, the wish is 'to defeat a particular opponent or competitor'. Then the wish becomes negative. In case of a one-to-one match, it is necessary to learn about the opponent's weaknesses and then, pounce on them. Learning this strategy is a part of the skill learning. So is this a negative wish or a positive wish? For example, in a badminton match in a major tournament, the players keenly observe the future opponents and find out the weaknesses and strengths. And then they decide how to attack those weak points (such as a weak backhand). Is this positive, healthy competition? Most of us will agree that it is a positive skill building.

But, suppose, it is a competition between two companies. One company A finds out about a weak spot in the opponent company B's product. And then, the company A launches an ad campaign to highlight the weak spot and malign the product, then is it a healthy competition? Arguably, it can still be considered a healthy competition because, then company B will take steps to rectify the weak spot – and become better in the process!

However, if one competitor takes steps to damage and weaken the opponent, then can it be considered a negative wish? But if this is so, then what will you say about a boxing match? The sport (?) involves hitting and weakening the opponent. Is it positive or negative?

Let us look at another basic wish: the 'wish to get respect / love from others'. Isn't it a positive wish? Even animals have this wish. But consider an arrogant alpha male who demands respect from a young adult male. The young adult male doesn't want to bow. So, a fight starts. And the loser has to surrender and show respect to winner in order to survive. Now, will you say that the 'wish to get respect from others' is a positive wish?

All of us work hard to achieve some status. One of the major reasons for this is to get respect from people. We also do a lot to give love – in order to get love. The result is so much satisfaction of getting respect and love. Then it is indeed a very positive wish.

But there are many humans who have the negative shade of this wish – just like the alpha males of the animals. Some of the religious and political leaders belong to this category. Respect is a big word for them. Slightest hint of disrespect and they (with their fanatic followers) start thrashing the people who don't respect the leader. We can see such people across the world.

Thus, a positive wish becomes a negative wish, when the person starts hurting others in order to fulfill the wish. The 'wish to enjoy sex' becomes a negative wish when it involves rape. The 'wish to create' (a book or a movie) becomes negative when it is created to hurt some people. Can you tell when a positive 'wish to own or possess' becomes negative?

It is not easy to decide which wish is positive and which wish is negative. Hence I have left many question marks for you to decide for yourself.

56

"Hey, buddy! Stop brooding"

When people consult me for their psychological problems, one my first few questions is: "Do you keep thinking of the problem again and again and again?" Most of the times, the answer is yes. This is not the result of their problems, but rather, the cause of their problems.

Of course, the repetitive thinking of happy thoughts does not trouble us. In fact, we become happier. And we get nice, prolonged satisfaction out of it. But, painful thoughts played again and again in the mind, can become a source of prolonged and intensified misery.

Thinking about a topic again and again is like inflating a balloon. The balloon is really small – just a few centimetres – to begin with. But every time we blow into it, it becomes bigger and bigger. Finally, it seems quite huge – quite out of proportion to the actual size of the balloon. Our problems are like that. They may be small to begin with. For example, a young man was lightly ridiculed in the office about finishing the work late. It was almost like the routine pulling of the legs and making fun of each other among friends. But the man, who was always very sincere and very perfect in his work, felt hurt. He went into brooding – endlessly thinking about 'why the colleagues ridiculed him, do they think like this about him behind his back, isn't it so unfair since he has always been good in his work, will it affect his promotion or worse, will it lead to him being sacked' – and so on and on.

These thoughts were important for him because they were 'emotional thoughts'. If a thought is emotional, it seems important to us. And because the thought is important, we keep thinking about it again and again – leading to the replay of associated emotions. This becomes a vicious cycle. But the main effect of this repetitive thinking is that, with every repetition, the emotion becomes more and more intense.

"I can't understand my daughter. Why does she have to keep thinking about the quarrel she had with her friend more than a week ago?" People who do not brood find it difficult to understand why some persons have out of proportion intense emotions about seemingly small problems. We keep reading or hearing about people who commit suicides after apparently small problems such as not-so-good marks or break-up or some such reasons. In such situations, emotional brooding is the culprit.

But why doesn't it happen every time with every person when a problem is encountered? What makes some people more prone to such brooding? If you have close friends or family members with whom you can share your pains, there is less likelihood of a brooding cycle setting up. People who have moved to a new town and have not made friends yet, face this problem. People, who feel that their problem is too personal to be shared with anyone, are in the same soup.

Actually, it is not even necessary to share the problem to break the brooding cycle. If the person gets fully involved in some other activity, the cycle breaks. For example, a young woman was caught in such a brooding trap after failing in an interview. I told her to go and play a vigorous game of badminton – since she was a badminton enthusiast. She did just that and the result was quite dramatic. "By the time I finished the game, my mind felt as light as a feather. The balloon burst. And I really started wondering why I was feeling so emotional about not getting that job. I can always get another one."

It was good that she could at least get involved in the game. Some of the people who get stuck in the brooding cycle are simply unable to divert their minds from the 'terribly important topic' – even if they or their dear ones try. For example, some people feel that removing every germ from their hands is so terribly important that they keep washing their hands endlessly and are unable to divert their mind to other topics. This is the condition called Obsessive Compulsive Disorder. Thus, brooding makes a normal person drift into the clutches of many disorders such as depression.

So what can be done to avoid this? Most importantly, recognize if you (or a near and dear one) is doing too much useless, unproductive brooding. If you feel you are, then talk to dear ones about the problem. Or, even if you don't feel like talking about your problem, simply talk to people to get some fresh, new thoughts into your mind. If you can get fully involved in some different activity, there is nothing like it. Any which way, prick the balloon and cut it down to size. Come back and address the problem later with a fresh mind.

57
Playing chess with Destiny

Destiny, with a crafty smile on face, said, "Check", and put Anita in a serious vehicular accident. But Anita is a fighter. She is not the one to give up easily. So, she made her moves and fought back - and freed herself from the 'check' – and the possible 'checkmate'! She is back in the game making her moves with relish every day.

She knows that a 'check' is not necessarily 'checkmate'. Many people don't realize this. For example, some people, who fail in an exam or get into a breakup, feel its checkmate – end of the game. But it is not so. There are many people who react in a similar fashion when they are told that they have diabetes or other health problems. Their reaction: "Now on it is living in the shadow of death. It is loss of all pleasures, so much trouble having to take medicines" etc. etc. But people like Anita don't lose their nerves when Destiny places a problem in their life's chessboard. They realize that life - like the game of chess - is a game of nerves. Those who don't lose their nerve do well and keep winning – in spite of the sharp attacks made by Destiny.

Anyone who has played chess knows that no two games are alike. The 32 pieces and 64 squares ensure practically infinite permutations and combinations of games. And so is the case with our lives. Each person's life is so completely different. Even the lives of siblings, who grow up in the same house and have the same parents, eventually, lead completely different lives. You, me and all of us play completely different games. So, it unwise to compare yourself and your life with others and their lives. Becoming unhappy because s/he has got such and such thing that I haven't got, is unwise!

It is very interesting to see a chess tournament where many matches are being played simultaneously. All the games begin with exactly the same starting positions of chess pieces on the board. Then see the games after just a few minutes and few moves – and each game is so completely different! And, just to compare, all of us begin our lives with completely different positions of pieces on the board! Our family backgrounds, our position in the same family, the advantages and disadvantages - are all different. So, obviously, each one's game is bound to be totally different. So, comparing and becoming unhappy is not at all a good idea.

But does it mean that we should stop comparing the games? Of course, not! All the great chess players keep studying the games played by others – but with the attitude of learning. They learn how others have faced and solved the tricky problems. But chess masters know that they cannot copy entire games (entire lives). They can only learn the solutions to specific problems. But it helps a lot. For example, suppose a businessman goes into a loss. Now, there are two possible reactions: one is to become sad by comparing his life with that of other successful businesspeople. The other is to meet or study businesspersons who have come out of loss – and learn from them. The point to be noted is that this person is not comparing whole lives but specific problem situation and learning the tricks that others have used.

The major difference between a great chess player and an ordinary chess player is in anticipating moves. It is about knowing how the opponent will react to your moves – and also, how the opponent is likely to attack. The ordinary player can anticipate only one or two moves that the opponent can make. The great player can see many moves ahead and then decide the best plan of action. Whether it is taking care of future financial health or body's health, we need to anticipate the possible moves by Destiny and plan our moves accordingly. Suppose you have hypertension but are feeling well otherwise. Then should you just ignore the BP or anticipate the future complications that the Destiny may place on your chessboard – and make your moves: checkups and following a healthy lifestyle (such as exercising)? Just like the game of chess, we can make anticipatory moves to stop many types of attacks from happening.

Every chess piece – King, Queen, Bishop, Rook, Knight, Pawn – has certain strengths – and weaknesses. This is just like all the people including you! Chess players don't complain that Knight cannot move straight or the Rook cannot jump over other pieces. It is best to accept the people as they are and play the game as well as possible.

Every day we plan our moves: I will do this, I will do that. But Destiny has a different plan. Sometimes we can anticipate Destiny's moves, but sometimes we get a complete surprise. Suddenly you get transferred, somebody falls ill, suddenly the school or government changes the rules and so on. Then we have to change our plan of attack and get into defensive mode to minimize the damage. Sometimes, what seems like Destiny's attack, turns out to be favourable to us – if we are adaptable and see the opportunity.

So, be cool and enjoy the game of chess with Destiny!

58

Confidently yours ...

A famous cricketer of yesteryears was known to be a very confident and attacking batsman. He would fearlessly go on the frontfoot and hit many sixes. But 2-3 times he got out early, while trying to hit sixes. There was severe criticism from all around. He was so shaken that he tried to change his game and adopted a defensive style of batting. The result was disastrous. Finally, a coach managed to bring back his confidence – and the attacking style, and he really came back to his original game.

One can see so many examples of brilliant students losing their confidence just before the major exam. The parents and teachers simply cannot understand why, a student who has done so well up to the prelims, should lose her / his confidence? Or consider the case of a bright - and even naughty - young person who became a lawyer. This person would lose all the confidence whenever there was a presentation in court. We all have seen intelligent students losing their confidence while giving a speech on stage.

What makes a person confident – and what causes a person to lose it? Confidence nothing but a prediction that, 'I will do well'. A simplistic logic states: if you are good at something, you will feel confident; if you are not good at something, you will feel a lack of confidence. Well, in most real life situations with real life people, there are many other factors that can change this equation.

Consider the sale force of a company. A smart alecky manager, who tries to appear smarter than others by pointing out mistakes of colleagues, does a lot of harm. Constant criticism of mistakes or underperformance undermines the confidence of the staff. They start fearing failures. When they go out to perform, they are reminded of their past mistakes – rather than past achievements. That gives a body blow to their confidence. On the other hand, the best manager is the one who criticizes while ensuring that the confidence is maintained by remembering the past glories.

One brilliant manager developed a wonderful policy. It would so happen that the big bosses would come to their department and criticize and then go away – leaving the colleagues licking their wounds. Then this great manager started using a 3 : 1 policy. Whenever a big boss came and started to fire his machine gun, this manager would describe his policy: "It is the policy of this department that before criticizing any person, you have to tell three good things about the person first." As you can understand, it made the bosses sensitive to what they were doing to the employees. And it was great boost to the confidence of the employees, who would show more receptiveness to the criticism – while feeling good about themselves!

A bad mood is a major shaker of the confidence. Suppose a player has had some problems at home or in relationships. Those problems may actually have nothing to do with the game or his skills. But that sad or fearful mood can shake the confidence. This is because, as said earlier, confidence is nothing but a prediction that, "I will do well". And, mood distorts this prediction. The result: loss of confidence. In this situation, the best policy would be to work on the root cause: change the mood to a happy, pleasant one. It works.

An extreme case of mood distorting the confidence is Obsessive Compulsive Disorder. The people who suffer from this, have a complete loss of confidence about their own basic actions. For example, normally people go and shut all the doors and latches at night. After this action, we are confident that we locked properly and we can sleep peacefully. But people who have OCD, do not feel confident that they have locked properly. So, they go and check again and again. They may do this action even 10-15 times. But when they are in a good mood, the confidence returns. So they feel secure after one or two checks.

The other extreme is the Supremely Confident Person! This person is always 100% sure of her / his every idea, every action! Even if this lay person is talking to an expert, s/he easily dismisses the experienced opinions of the expert. This leads to a lot of frustration in people who deal with this person. All of us have seen bratty children who become a nuisance wherever they go – and yet are never, ever disciplined by their parents. These children grow up into the Supremely Confident Persons!

What about the situation when you know that you really don't have enough skills? Can you work confidently in this situation? The answer is 'Yess'! It is possible to develop an attitude of confidence – irrespective of the situation. Some people call it by the funny oxymoron: Confidence in incompetence! But, yes, this attitude really helps to give one's best performance in tough situations.

59
Is it a scratch, a fracture or a heart attack?

Miss. N. was getting ready for the big party in her college. She had planned her dress since many days. On the day, she took out the dress. And, oops! There was a big hole in the front of the dress. All hell broke loose. Panic, bomb-blasts, threat of revenge, crying, national record for fastest emptying of the entire cupboard – all elements of high drama present!

The big question is: Is such an intense emotional outburst proportional to the degree of the problem? Is it too much? The question is: Is it a scratch-level problem or a fracture-level problem of a heart attack-level problem?

All of us go through several small and big problems every day. And as a result, we keep on getting various emotions in various intensities. We naturally expect that each emotion should be proportional to the magnitude of the problem. This is especially true for the unhappy emotions: sadness, fear and anger. Happiness is different. A little plus or minus of happiness does not make much difference. But excess of sadness, fear or anger makes a lot of difference for the person - and for the people around.

One important part of 'growing up' is responding with a proper intensity of emotion. For example, consider a tiny tot. He is playing with a toy happily. Another child (or even an adult with a naughty intention) comes and snatches the toy. The child starts crying at the top of his voice – with the maximum intensity the child can muster! It is obvious that the intensity of the emotional reaction is quite out of proportion to the degree of the problem. As children 'grow up', they come know that it is not a life and death problem. So, they realize that it is not a 'heart attack grade' problem or even a 'fracture grade problem' – but only a 'scratch grade' one.

This scale of 'scratch – fracture – heart attack' is very useful to grade one's problems. Most of the times, we don't have an easy scale available for judging how severe a problem is. Every person feels that the problem s/he is going through is the worst type of unbearable problem that anyone can ever face. The issue may be anything: breakup of a couple, pimples of a teenager, failure in an exam, losing a wallet of a few thousand rupees or insult by an office colleague and so on. When a person becomes emotional, the problem seems unbearable. And hence the intensity of the emotion seems justified.

This is one peculiar property of the mind: often, we judge the severity of a problem by looking at the emotional reaction it has generated – and not by objectively looking at the severity of the problem. Listen to someone describing 'how insulting the behavior of a colleague was'. If you observe that the person is feeling deeply hurt and emotional, you are likely to conclude that the insult was indeed terrible. However, if the person was not emotional while describing the insult, you are likely to conclude that the insult was not so bad. The point to be noted is that the emotional reaction can vary – depending on whether the person was already depressed or not etc. So, the emotional reaction of a depressed person can be excessive or out of proportion to the severity of the problem.

In such situations, our scale of 'scratch – fracture – heart attack' becomes very useful to objectively understand how bad the problem is. Then we can tone down our emotional response to the appropriate level.

The brave and calm people typically show a more controlled or less severe emotional reaction – even when facing a serious problem. They don't panic or start crying or blow up with anger when faced with – even heart attack level problems. Their calmness helps them to face the situation better. This is a great asset.

But showing a less emotional reaction can be troublesome, too. Suppose, a wife is telling the husband about some 'terrible' problem that she had. Now, if the husband remains calm and less emotional, the wife may think that the husband is a heartless person who does not care for her problems. In such situations an appropriately intense emotional response is necessary.

An out of proportion emotional reaction is a hallmark of many disorders such as depression, anxiety, phobias or anger problems. For example, consider blood phobia. Whenever a person, who has this problem, sees blood s/he emotionally reacts as if a most terrifying event has happened – sometimes leading to fainting. Stage fright troubles so many people. It is an out of proportion fear related to some possible negative comments by the audience.

If such a person applies the 'scratch – fracture – heart attack' scale to the problem, s/he will realize that it is only a scratch level problem. This scale has helped so many people. You can also try it.

60
'Switch off' the problems for some time

A man was telling his friend, "In my house, my wife takes all the SMALL decisions: Which school should the children go to, where should we go for the vacation, which car should we buy etc. And I take all the BIG decisions: Which batsman should open the inning for India, which country should the PM visit, who should become the President of the USA etc." Joke apart, this points to a very important and common activity that all of us indulge in: getting fully involved in issues that are not connected to us directly. These include international politics, sports where we are not personally involved, debates on the TV about national events, interesting happenings in remote countries etc. And, yes, the man did not realize that his wife, too, is involved in making similar BIG decisions: how should all the characters in her favourite TV serials behave, what should different celebrities wear for different grand occasions, how should her office colleague's neighbour's sister-in-law behave with her mother-in-law etc. Are all these activities just *faaltu* timepass? Or do they serve any important purpose in our lives?

Of course, they are very useful activities! Such activities and animated discussions and even, just watching such things on TV, serve an important purpose: for some time, at least, they take our minds off our routine day-to-day life. This is no small achievement! Once, some of my friends were discussing movies. One serious friend said, "Movies should be realistic and have some message". Another friend said, "Spectacular, exotic fantasies are very important. Such movies can make ordinary people, who are burdened by their problems, forget those problems for some time. And it's a very a noble work". Many such movies – especially the ones with happy endings – give a lot of happiness and hope and freshness of the mind to all the millions of viewers. When viewers come out of the movie hall with laugher and happiness, it's a great achievement.

All of us have the daily dose of problems – small or big. The solvable problems don't cause a lot of misery. We solve them and get on with life. But there are many, many problems that are unsolvable or are going to take a long time to get solved. The mind has a tendency to keep on thinking about such problems again and again - almost endlessly. Then the mind starts suffering – a very prolonged suffering. Apparently, the mind keeps searching for solutions. But we know fairly well that some problems (such as death of a loved one) do not have a solution. Some problems (such as business losses) do not have a quick solution. The mind almost reaches the point of fatigue thinking about them again and again. That is the time to switch off the problems – at least for some time.

This 'switching off the problems for some time' has many benefits. It removes the mind's fatigue and makes it fresh again – ready to take on the challenges of life! Normally, a good sleep can do this job. But some unfortunate people are not able get sound, refreshing sleep. For them, such switching off is immensely useful.

You must have observed this: suppose, you are stuck with some tricky problem. You keep on thinking about it, but are unable to think of a solution. Then you get involved in some totally unrelated activity for some time. And afterwards, you come back to the original problem. Many a times, we find that when we approach the problem with a refreshed mind, we suddenly get the answer!

For many people, such switching off means a long awaited relief. We can see many elderly couples in whom one person is bed-ridden or dependent – while the other person is reasonably fit. Being caring persons, the fit elderly takes on the responsibility of caring for the other. But 24*7 caring leads to mental tiredness. If other members of the family recognize this, they ensure that this care-giver gets a much needed vacation to remove the burden from the mind.

Vacations are great from the switching off point of view. It means a complete change of scene: different house, different food, different people and different pleasures! It's a big switch off from the same old daily routine. But it involves spending a lot of time – and money! So it can be done once in a while – but not every day!

It is necessary for each of us to find some activity that can be done every day. For different people, the activities can be quite different. The hobbies are actually great switch offs. For example, singing, gardening, reading, cooking and so on and on.

It is essential that the activity grabs your attention. Only then, it can serve as switch off. If the activity has become routine and boring, it cannot serve as a switch off. Then, it is time to find another activity.

So, what are you waiting for? Switch on the Idiot box – oops, the smart, 'switch off' box – get transported to another world – for some time!

About Author

~ Alumnus of the Seth G. S. Medical College (KEM Hospital), Parel, Mumbai

~ Member of the Indian Psychiatric Society, Bombay Psychiatric Society, Indian Medical Association

~ Presented several research papers in national and international Psychiatric conferences

~ Published several research papers in national and international Psychiatric and Psychology journals

~ Nearly three decades of experience of treating patients using counselling and medicines

Other interests:

~ Involved in saving birds. Made a documentary called 'Our Birds' and presented more than hundred live commentary shows of the same

~ One of the Founder Members of the erstwhile Humour Club Bombay